Improving Undergraduate Education Through Faculty Development

An Analysis of Effective Programs and Practices

Kenneth E. Eble

Wilbert J. McKeachie

Improving Undergraduate Education Through Faculty Development

Jossey-Bass Publishers

San Francisco • London • 1986

IMPROVING UNDERGRADUATE EDUCATION THROUGH FACULTY
DEVELOPMENT
An Analysis of Effective Programs and Practices
by Kenneth E. Eble and Wilbert J. McKeachie

Copyright © 1985 by: Jossey-Bass Inc., Publishers
433 California Street
San Francisco, California 94104
&
Jossey-Bass Limited
28 Banner Street
London EC1Y 8QE

LB
2331.73
,M6
E24
1985

Library of Congress Cataloging in Publication Data

Eble, Kenneth Eugene.
Improving undergraduate education through faculty
development.

(Jossey-Bass higher education series)
Bibliography: p. 235
Includes index.
1. College teachers—In-service training—Minnesota—
Case studies. 2. College teachers—In-service training
—North Dakota—Case studies. 3. College teachers—
In-service training—South Dakota—Case studies.
I. McKeachie, Wilbert James (date). II. Title.
III. Series.
LB2331.73.M6E24   1985   370'.7'124   84-43027
ISBN 0-87589-643-X

Manufactured in the United States of America

The paper in this book meets the guidelines for
permanence and durability of the Committee on
Production Guidelines for Book Longevity of the
Council on Library Resources.

JACKET DESIGN BY WILLI BAUM

FIRST EDITION
First printing: April 1985
Second printing: April 1986

Code 8512

The Jossey-Bass
Higher Education Series

Preface

The Bush Foundation Faculty Development Project in Minnesota and the Dakotas, begun in 1980, afforded an unusual opportunity to study faculty development at close hand and within a variety of collegiate institutions. The project embraced virtually all the colleges in the region, from denominational colleges with barely 500 students to the University of Minnesota with over 55,000. The Foundation's aim was to improve undergraduate education; the programs supported by Foundation funds enabled faculty members at each institution to engage in activities deemed useful to that larger purpose. The result was a diversity of over thirty separate programs, each initially funded for three years. Twenty-four of those programs had completed the initial three-year cycle by the time this book was completed. Thanks to more recently awarded initial and renewal grants, program activities will continue through the 1980s.

Most of the Bush programs have been renewed for an

additional three-year period with the hope that they might be substantially carried on after that period by institutional funds. Although at this writing no programs have come to the end of their six-year period of Foundation support, a number of institutions have taken over some of the funding of program activities. A check of twenty-six institutions disclosed that twenty-four were projecting spending levels for faculty development after the end of Foundation support that represented an increase over spending levels before the Bush program began. Foundation guidelines emphasized the shaping of proposals by the institutions themselves, and while programs varied, most included activities common to faculty development everywhere. Grants to individual faculty members for further study, for revising courses, for developing teaching skills, and for preparing new courses were a part of most programs. Many programs included workshops and seminars of various kinds. Some supported visiting scholars, teachers, and consultants. Some brought faculty and students together as partners in research. Internal evaluations were a part of all programs.

This varied and closely observed program of activities provided the basic material for this study. The Foundation's entry into faculty development was a new venture, and one that resulted, to a high degree, in faculty development built from perceived individual and institutional needs rather than from an outside design. As the project developed, the advisability of supplementing the individual program evaluations with an overall evaluation of the project became apparent.

In the summer of 1982, the authors of this book were commissioned to perform this evaluation. Kenneth Eble had previously been a consultant to the Foundation for the project and a site visitor for many of the individual proposals. Wilbert McKeachie had not been previously involved with the project but had conducted many related projects and studies. His activities were particularly focused on designing the evaluative questionnaire, developing theoretical propositions, and collecting and analyzing data from faculty and administration. In addition he made site visits to most of the colleges and universities with Bush-supported programs. The shaping of the book and the conclusions reached resulted from a close collaboration between the two authors. The Bush Foundation was generous in providing the time of their staff and consultants and in supporting all our efforts at overall evaluation. We profited greatly from the documentary material they provided, discussions with staff, and staff review of our drafts. At the same time, they left us free to follow our own methodologies and to arrive at our own conclusions.

We were also interested, as was the Foundation, in contributing to the study of faculty development, which has produced a substantial body of material, much of it within the last decade. Throughout the book, we have tried to connect our findings with respect to this sample with faculty development at large. We have emphasized the implications of programs and activities in these colleges and universities for similar institutions elsewhere. Presidents and academic affairs officers, deans and department chairpersons, faculty members at large as well as those specifically involved in faculty development should be usefully informed by our findings.

The contents of this study are presented in three parts. Part One, comprising the first four chapters, sets forth the nature and purposes of faculty development and describes the Bush Foundation's Faculty Development Program overall and the activities supported by it in participating colleges and universities.

Chapter One discusses faculty development in the United States and reviews its history with particular attention to efforts being made in the last fifteen years. Perhaps because traditional faculty development support emphasized research, the emphasis in more recent years has been on developing instructional competence. The chapter reviews the substantial literature that examines various developmental activities—instructional, curricular, and organizational—that are closely related to the professional development of individual faculty members. The chapter ends with a discussion of the importance of adjusting faculty development efforts to fit faculty and institutional needs.

Chapter Two describes some of the major efforts made by private foundations in support of faculty development. External funding has been an important source of such support, for institutional funds tend to be concentrated on providing the basic salaries, fringe benefits, and working conditions necessary for instruction and scholarship. The involvement of the Bush Foundation in supporting higher education is described and related to the inception of its Faculty Development Program. From its past experience and awareness of conditions affecting faculty and students, the Foundation evolved a program aimed ultimately at improving undergraduate learning by assisting the faculty in ways that the faculty of individual colleges and universities might propose.

Chapters Three and Four present brief descriptions of the institutions in this study and their faculty development programs. For convenience of presentation, institutions are grouped either as privately supported colleges and universities, in Chapter Three, or as publicly supported ones, in Chapter Four. They are presented in alphabetical order in each chapter so that the reader can quickly turn to any specific college or university and find a brief sketch of the institution and a summary description of its faculty development program.

Part Two, Chapters Five through Eight, provides a detailed analysis of faculty development efforts through a number of case studies of faculty development programs at selected institutions. The colleges and universities described were chosen because they represent certain kinds and sizes of institutions, both public and private, and the programs they developed. These case studies are both descriptive and analytical. Their intent is not to call attention to the institutions identified and their faculty development efforts but rather to suggest to colleges and universities of similar kinds considerations useful to their own efforts at faculty development.

Part Three, Chapters Nine through Eleven, analyzes the effectiveness of faculty development programs from a number of perspectives. Chapter Nine looks at faculty across our sample of institutions largely from a questionnaire circulated to a random sampling of the entire faculty cohort. It came as something of a surprise to find that satisfactions among the faculty in this sample were high at a time of supposedly widespread dissatisfaction nationally.

Chapter Ten describes in detail our methods of evaluation and discusses the difficulties of program evaluations of this kind. Despite the difficulties, and specifically those encountered in making this study, we conclude that useful evaluations can be made, even those extending into whether student learning is actually affected by changes in faculty behavior, attitude, and performance.

Chapter Eleven sets forth our conclusions. In general, they endorse the overall success of the Bush program and point to specific characteristics that account for that success. Equally important, this final chapter draws attention to the kinds of faculty development activities and ways of carrying them out that should be useful to a wide range of colleges and universities.

The support and cooperation we received as evaluators of this project was a continuation of the support and cooperation that was marked in the conduct of the project itself. The use of consultants and their availability to applicant institutions has been generous. A sense of common commitment to improving student learning, often a gratifying aspect of site visits, has been as present among the Foundation staff, advisers, and consultants as among faculty and administrators of individual institutions. Submitted proposals have been carefully prepared and amplified in great detail. Site visits to all institutions have been a regular part of the granting process, and mid-grant visits have been made to a number of institutions. Networking activities were established early in the project's history and considerable evidence exists that the project has created a useful regional identity so that programs at one institution have had an impact on programs at another.

In conclusion, we wish to repeat that this is an independent study; the responsibility for its accuracy, thoroughness, and conclusions rests solely with us. We wish to thank the staff of the Bush Foundation, Humphrey Doermann, Stanley Shepard, and John Archabal, with whom we have worked closely and collegially, in the best sense. The Foundation has been both generous in its support and zealous in leaving us free to proceed as we wished and to such conclusions as we might reach. We wish also to thank the many individuals on the many campuses who contributed time, insights, and data to this study.

We wish particularly to thank Robert Blackburn, Paul Dressel, Paul Lacey, B. Claude Mathis, and Dean Whitla, who read the manuscript and contributed many valuable suggestions. Special thanks go to Dorothy L. Cameron, who was a partner in this venture from July 1983 through April 1984, managing data collection, participating in site visits, and planning data analysis and interpretation. We are also grateful to Yi-Guang Lin, who managed computer analyses of the data, and to Daniel Byk, Angie Dahl, Tania Fak, and Brian Tishuk, our research assistants. Thanks also to Melissa Eble, Genevieve Rowe, and Laura J. Liebler, who patiently and cheerfully prepared various drafts of the manuscript.

February 1985   Kenneth E. Eble
                                                 Salt Lake City, Utah

                                                 Wilbert J. McKeachie
                                                 Ann Arbor, Michigan

Contents

The Authors

Kenneth E. Eble is professor of English and University Professor at the University of Utah, Salt Lake City. He received his B.A. and M.A. degrees from the University of Iowa (1948, 1949) and his Ph.D. degree in English from Columbia University (1956).

Eble began teaching at Upper Iowa University in 1949 and also taught at the Columbia School of General Studies (1951-54) and Drake University (1954-55) before joining the faculty at the University of Utah in 1955. From 1964 to 1969, he was chairman of the English department at the University of Utah, taking leave from 1969 to 1971 to direct the Project to Improve College Teaching, cosponsored by the American Association of University Professors (AAUP) and the Association of American Colleges and funded by the Carnegie Corporation.

During the past fifteen years, Eble has frequently been a guest speaker and consultant on teaching and faculty development at more than 200 colleges and universities in the United

States and Canada. He has served in many official positions within the AAUP, the Modern Language Association, the National Council of Teachers of English, and Phi Beta Kappa.

Eble's writing has embraced not only education but American literature, the humanities, history of ideas, and popular culture. In addition to *Professors as Teachers* (1972), *The Craft of Teaching: A Guide to Mastering the Professor's Art* (1976), *The Art of Administration* (1978), and *The Aims of College Teaching* (1983), Eble's books include *Old Clemens and W.D.H.* (1985), *William Dean Howells* (1982), *F. Scott Fitzgerald* (rev. ed. 1976), *The Profane Comedy* (1962), *A Perfect Education* (1966), and, as editor, *Howells: A Century of Criticism* (1962) and *The Intellectual Tradition of the West* (1967). He is a field editor for the Twayne United States Author Series and editor of the Jossey-Bass sourcebook *New Directions for Teaching and Learning.*

Wilbert J. McKeachie is professor of psychology and former director of the Center for Research on Learning and Teaching at the University of Michigan where he has spent his entire professional career since taking his doctorate in 1949. His primary activities have been college teaching, research on college teaching, and training college teachers.

He is past president of the American Psychological Association, the American Association of Higher Education, and the American Psychological Foundation. He is also past chairman of the Committee on Teaching, Research, and Publication of the American Association of University Professors. Currently he is president of the Division of Educational, Instructional, and School Psychology of the International Association of Applied Psychology. He has been a member of various governmental advisory committees on mental health, behavioral and biological research, and graduate training.

He has written a number of books and articles including *Teaching Tips: A Guidebook for the Beginning College Teacher* (1978).

He has received honorary degrees from Northwestern University, Denison University, Eastern Michigan University, and the University of Cincinnati.

Improving Undergraduate Education Through Faculty Development

An Analysis
of Effective Programs
and Practices

Part One

Nature and Purpose
of Faculty
Development Programs

Preliminary to our specific evaluation of the Bush Foundation Faculty Development Program is our review of faculty development efforts in the United States. This review includes a look at sabbatical leaves, the traditional form of professional development, at efforts to improve instruction, at curriculum development and reform, and at organizational change. Foundations are important to these activities, for they not only perceive higher education from a different perspective but also provide funds that are not easily forthcoming from within the institution for a range of activities that favorably affect faculty performance.

The Bush Foundation is only one of a number of major foundations that have supported extensive faculty development efforts in the last fifteen years. Like most foundations, its assistance to higher education has taken diverse forms. Building on previous experience in assisting colleges and universities, the Foundation's faculty development program evolved in the context of widespread faculty development activities nationally and of the need to offset conditions adversely affecting both faculty and students. Our intention in the first two chapters of this section is not to present a full review of faculty development gen-

1

erally nor to explore thoroughly the involvement of private
foundations in faculty development. Rather, it is to provide
some of the background out of which the specifics of the Bush
Faculty Development Program emerged.

What is distinctive about the Bush program is that it is
not a centrally administered program affecting college and university faculties in a set way but rather the aggregation of
individual faculty development programs shaped by each institution's efforts to identify opportunities and needs and to propose a variety of ways of serving both. Since the program is
extensive and diverse, we have in Chapters Three and Four provided brief sketches of the privately and publicly supported
colleges and universities involved and of the faculty development programs in each. The colleges and universities in Chapter
Three are alphabetically arranged in three groups in accordance
with size of full-time enrollments: up to 1,000 students, 1,000
to 3,000 students, and more than 3,000 students. The publicly
supported institutions include programs supported by grants
made to individual colleges and universities but also individual
programs at institutions within a state system for which funding
was provided in a grant to that system. At the end of each chapter, we make brief observations about these programs, but extensive analysis is reserved for the case studies that comprise
Part Two, Chapters Five through Eight, of this study.

✣ 1 ✣

Evolution of Faculty
Development Efforts

Faced with declining and changing enrollment patterns, increased requirements for accountability, declining financial resources, and a faculty adversely affected by these and other
conditions, many colleges and universities in the 1970s turned
to faculty development as a major responsibility. Demographic
studies indicate that as we move toward the year 2000, college-
age populations in many areas of the country will continue to
support few openings with tenure opportunities for college faculty in many disciplines. Some departments will have an over-
supply of faculty while others will find it difficult to hire
enough qualified faculty to meet student demands. Retirements
of the large age cohort that expanded faculties in the 1960s will
probably modify these predictions. In general, existing faculties
will have grown older and will have less job mobility. The modal
age of tenured faculty by the year 2000 is estimated to be between fifty-six and sixty-five. In 1981, that modal age range was
thirty-six to forty-five (Chait and Ford, 1982).

　　With respect to students, educators predict fewer traditional students, increased minority and female enrollments, and
an increased commitment to lifelong learning. Moreover, students are greatly affected by an awareness of shifts in kinds of
jobs, pressures to find and prepare for jobs and careers, and the
impact of technology on their lives and work. The traditions of

liberal arts education have a weak hold, and the worth of college going itself is under some suspicion. The search for a common core of undergraduate studies goes on in almost every institution. At the same time many faculties must contend with the imbalances created by shifts in enrollments from one area to another.

Given these conditions, it is not surprising to find that faculty development established itself in the 1970s (Centra, 1976). By 1976, Centra's survey disclosed that 60 percent of the U.S. institutions that responded had programs for faculty development or instructional improvement. The approaches used were diverse, focusing on learning, teaching, instruction, and, to a lesser degree, on the personal and professional development of the faculty.

Background of Faculty Development

The more surprising fact about faculty development is not its rapid rise, but that it should have occupied so little attention in the past. Universities long ago modeled themselves on business practices, and no successful business could prosper without committing large sums to development of its major resources. True, the emphasis upon human resources in business management is a somewhat recent development. But for colleges and universities, even those most concerned with physical facilities, the human resources—the faculty and supporting personnel—have long been their most important and expensive resources.

A brief and tentative answer to why colleges and universities have not long embraced faculty development begins with the fact that teachers at that level are primarily concerned with scholarly study in a disciplinary area. As Light (1984) and others have pointed out, academics tend to be professionals in their discipline but not necessarily in teaching. College teaching tends to be a profession in which secondary attention is given to teaching itself. If public schooling has been criticized for forcing its practitioners through a program in which pedagogy looms large, college and university teaching is equally chargeable for fostering programs in which pedagogy is scarcely present.

If there is so little recognition of the "teaching" competences of professionals entering the field, there is likely to be little recognition of the need to develop established faculty as teachers. Institutional practices in support of their faculties have largely, almost exclusively, been in support of research or scholarly capacities. The sabbatical leave, begun at Harvard in 1810 (Blackburn, Pellino, Boberg, and O'Connell, 1980), is the oldest form of faculty support. Its origins have both a theoretical and practical bent. At Harvard and at the handful of other American colleges that existed before the Civil War, leaves were sometimes given to enable the prospective professor to gain sufficient competence to teach a subject. When Bowdoin College trustees decided to add modern languages to their curricula—only William and Mary, Harvard, and Virginia had such—they hired the college's own recent graduate, Henry Wadsworth Longfellow, and sent him on a three-year sojourn in Europe to prepare himself. In 1834, when he accepted the Smith Professorship of Modern Languages at Harvard, the offer carried a suggestion that he spend another year or so in Europe to perfect his German. By 1842, for reasons of health as well as fatigue from his teaching duties, he took a leave of absence in the spring, but Harvard would not extend his paid leave into that fall (Arvin, 1963).

Throughout the nineteenth century, the sabbatical was one of those seeming privileges that enhanced a genteel profession. Rudolph (1977) relates the growth of paid leaves of absence and sabbatical years to the growth of research and scholarly publishing characteristic of the 1890s and following decades. Ingraham's (1965) survey of faculty benefits found that just under 60 percent of the universities and fewer than 40 percent of the colleges granted paid leaves other than sabbaticals. Of the total of 745 four-year colleges within and separate from universities, 57 percent granted sabbaticals. In 1965, the typical sabbatical was a half year at full pay or a full year at half pay. These findings are supported by a survey (Eble, 1972) made in 1970 that found that only about 60 percent of four-year institutions had sabbatical plans and that even fewer provided full funding for the year or placed no restrictions on the faculty member's use of time.

Whatever its origins and actualities, the sabbatical was clearly related to enhancing or renewing the scholar's capacities. Ingraham (1965, p. 72) stated, "The fact is clear that the chief purpose for leaves in the university is for research, writing, and study at the level of a trained active scholar." He also pointed out that the most frequent reason for extended leaves from the four-year college was for a faculty member to pursue advanced graduate work aimed at attaining the doctorate. As the research model became the standard one for major universities and as it affected faculty practices at most colleges, the sabbatical often became tied to specific research projects. In general, sabbaticals were competitive and given for research projects that could not be pursued on the professor's home campus and that required both travel and free time. Sabbaticals were neither designed nor supported for the purpose of improving pedagogical skills.

In more recent years, other scholarly and creative activities have become eligible for sabbatical support. Among the top institutions and their top faculty, sabbaticals and support for scholarly work are generally available even in today's constrained budgets; in hard-pressed private schools and public institutions, however, such benefits are less evident.

In a 1972 survey done under American Association of University Professors (AAUP) auspices (Eble, 1972), faculty members from 142 different institutions were almost unanimous in responding negatively to the main question, "My institution (does, does not) have an effective faculty development system." In response to the second question, "Outside of the departmental program and budget, my institution provides specific support for (research, teaching, service)," about 60 percent of the respondents reported specific support for research. About 10 percent reported specific support for teaching, and even fewer for service. Eighteen respondents reported that their institution offered no support outside the department budgets for research, teaching, or service, and little support within the department.

These findings at the end of the sixties were consistent with findings arising from an earlier survey of small colleges in the South (Miller and Wilson, 1963, p. 70): "While there are activities in these colleges directed toward establishing or improving approaches to faculty development, these activities are, in the main, uncoordinated and lacking in creativity . . . Often reliance is placed on a limited number of relatively routine procedures and emphasis tends to be placed on procedures related to the process of orienting faculty members to the institution—an important but limited aspect of the process of development." Among the "relatively routine procedures" were financial assistance for attending professional meetings, conferences or workshops, and for visiting lecturers or consultants on teaching; load adjustments for research and writing; lighter loads for first-year faculty members; and financial assistance to complete work on advanced degrees.

Except for favorable treatment shown to first-year teachers, none of these practices directly affects teaching. Attendance at some professional meetings might well enhance teaching; attendance at others would contribute little. The standard way of getting travel money is to read a paper at a professional meeting; most often the paper is not well-suited—in subject, language, style, and manner of presentation—to the students the professor is actually teaching. The presupposition in most of these practices is that development of greater command over a subject matter will contribute to the faculty member's general competence, of which teaching is one aspect. Even if we grant that somewhat shaky assumption, the nature of institutional support tends to slight teaching, to divert the faculty member's already fragmented attention away from the classroom, students, and learning. Few schools pay conscious attention to the ways in which faculty members develop as teachers, sustain their efforts, or decline.

It is granted that most colleges and universities give at least routine or sporadic attention to teaching. Teaching awards, for example, exist on many campuses as do formal and informal groups of faculty whose main interest is in teaching. Curriculum committees exist within most departments and concern themselves with this important aspect of instruction. Disciplinary associations, which have much to do with shaping faculty attitudes and practices, also demonstrate a secondary interest in teaching. In some instances, somewhat parallel organizations exist: the Modern Languages Association and the National Council of Teachers of English, for instance, or the American Institute of Chemical Engineers and the American Society for Mechanical Engineers as related to the American Society for Engineering Education. Publications focusing on teaching also occupy a secondary position as compared with the journals devoted to disciplinary research. Some examples are *Engineering Education, The Physics Teacher, Teaching Political Science,* the *Journal of Chemical Education,* and the *Teaching of Psychology.* Still, these associations and publications have less prestige than those devoted to disciplinary scholarship, and many institutions offer little in the way of specific support for faculty members wishing to develop as teachers.

Practices today are probably not very different from those revealed by surveys of a decade and two decades ago. A detailed survey (Fink, 1984) of the first year of teaching of 100 geography professors during the years 1976–1978 revealed an almost total absence of any measures that might have assisted the new faculty members during the first year. Only one in five of the new teachers in major universities thought they had lighter teaching loads than more experienced faculty, and two in five thought they had heavier.

Assisting beginning teachers has always had a low priority among faculty development efforts and this despite the obvious usefulness of supporting a person at the beginning of a career. An implication of the Fink study may be that faculty development efforts of the seventies were chiefly concerned with revitalizing existing faculty. Declining enrollments, smaller numbers of new faculty, and general passivity of the seventies created a fear of a "stagnant" faculty that development efforts might counter.

In sum, one must recognize that faculty development has never had a prominent place in the routine budgets of American collegiate institutions. Customary support for faculty development has not been primarily directed toward improving teaching, and while an increase in faculty development activities in the seventies did aim at developing faculty members as teachers, such activities are currently less well supported. Moreover, when faculty members are given a choice about what might best further their professional development, they gravitate toward conventional support—time off and travel funds—of their own research.

The impetus for placing an emphasis upon teaching surely came from the sheer size as well as the criticism from the undergraduate student body in the 1960s. Student evaluations, which have had their ups and downs at least since the 1920s, were closely linked with faculty development. From 1969 to 1971, the AAUP and the Association of American Colleges (AAC) received Carnegie Foundation funding to conduct a two-year Project to Improve College Teaching. The most effective parts of that work were those that helped bring student evaluations into widespread use and that called for more systematic "career development of college teachers," clearly a predecessor to the faculty development movement. The two were linked in the AAUP-AAC Project, for it was felt that by identifying and evaluating teaching skills, ways might also be found to assist faculty in acquiring further teaching competence. The pressures on faculty to adopt more effective ways of evaluating teaching also gave faculty a strong argument for asking for specific and greater support for faculty development.

As faculty development became an identifiable activity on many campuses, it took on a familiar professional identity. Networking organizations developed, articles and books described models and practices, and centers for research and practical application developed at a number of universities. Of the latter, the Center for Research on Learning and Teaching at the University of Michigan preceded most of the others by several years.

More directly related to recent interest in developing teaching competence among the faculty are various centers established both by institutional and outside funding. Such centers and offices are to be found at public and private universities, such as Colorado State, Illinois, Memphis State, Syracuse, University of Tennessee, and the University of Texas, to name

only a few. Among major foundation efforts of this kind are
the Center for the Teaching Professions established by the Kellogg Foundation at Northwestern University and the Centers for
Learning and Teaching established by the Danforth Foundation
at Harvard and Stanford. The activities of the Office of Education's Fund for the Improvement of Postsecondary Education
can also be mentioned as a recent federal effort to foster faculty
and instructional development. This by no means acknowledges
all the efforts at faculty development going on now or in the recent past; so numerous were these that the Professional and
Organizational Development Network in Higher Education
came into being to provide professional identity and activities
for individuals engaged in faculty development work.

Books and Classification of Faculty Development

Among the many books that defined and disseminated
ideas and practices are *Professors as Teachers* (Eble, 1972), *Faculty Development in a Time of Retrenchment* (Group for Human Development in Higher Education, 1974), *Toward Faculty
Renewal: Advances in Faculty, Instructional, and Organizational Development* (Gaff, 1975), *A Handbook for Faculty Development* (Bergquist, Phillips, and Quehl, 1975, 1977), *Faculty
Development Practices in U.S. Colleges and Universities* (Centra,
1976), *Faculty Development and Evaluation in Higher Education* (Smith, 1976), *Professional Development: A Guide to Resources* (Gaff, Festa, and Gaff, 1978), *Designing Teacher Improvement Programs* (Lindquist, 1979), *Renewal of the Teacher
Scholar: Faculty Development in the Liberal Arts College* (Nelsen, 1981), *Expanding Faculty Options: Career Development
Projects at Colleges and Universities* (Baldwin and others, 1981),
and *New Directions for Teaching and Learning: Revitalizing
Teaching Through Faculty Development* (Lacey, 1983).

These books and related articles provide much information about faculty development activities. A number attempt to
sort and classify faculty development efforts. Though theoriz-
ing chiefly about human motivation and adult development is
not absent in this literature, most of the content focuses on

practices. Gaff (1975) usefully places faculty development within larger efforts to improve collegiate instruction:

- *Faculty development:* programs to promote faculty growth, to help faculty members acquire knowledge, skills, and sensitivities
- *Instructional development:* programs that facilitate student learning, prepare learning materials, and redesign courses
- *Organizational development:* programs to create an effective organizational environment for teaching and learning

Bergquist, Phillips, and Quehl's (1975) description of faculty development closely parallels Gaff's model. They include *curriculum development* as another identifiable category.

One comment needs to be made about these classifications and the practices that bring them into being. *Faculty development* is both a comprehensive term that covers a wide range of activities ultimately designed to improve student learning and a less broad term that describes a purposeful attempt to help faculty members improve their competence as teachers and scholars. In this latter sense, the term refers to intentions and activities about which faculty are very sensitive, for they proceed from the assumption that many faculty members are in need of developing and they propose to adopt specific ways of going about it. Most institutions proceed cautiously with these activities. Commonly, the means are chosen by the faculty and take the form of such assistance as released time, travel grants, workshops and seminars, and the like. Occasionally they include more direct efforts to improve teaching skills through peer observing and counseling, videotaping, or specific action-oriented workshops. A so-called clinical approach may go beyond giving individual help in course design or similar instructional problems and attempt to change attitudes, clarify values, and develop interpersonal skills.

Though such activities overlap with those of instructional development, they preserve useful distinctions. *Instructional development* is both a more neutral term and a blanket term under which the emphasis is upon the instructional situation rather than upon faculty competence. Even though a workshop on the use of computers in instruction might involve the development of teaching skills, it would have a place in instructional development along with preparing learning materials or enlarging and improving the role of technology in instruction. Colleges and universities with a reluctance to attempt to affect faculty teaching directly may adopt instructional development as a preferred strategy.

Organizational development rather clearly separates itself from these other activities. It is also probably the hardest to bring about. If, as described by Gaff, it strenuously tried "to create an effective organizational environment for teaching and learning," it would question most of the traditional practices and patterns that define higher education. The division into departments, the academic calendar, the system of grades and credits, the conduct of athletics, the design of classrooms and buildings—all those structures that foster and restrict learning—would come under examination. If institutions are cautious about developing faculty, they are even more so in confronting the conventional structures that so affect teaching and learning. The autonomy of departments and their conventional clustering into separate colleges is a formidable barrier to organizational development. Some few colleges and universities have broken away from conventional structures but none of these innovative structures has been widely copied. Developing interdisciplinary courses and programs, team teaching, turning to competency-based instruction, and creating an office or organization to support faculty development itself are some activities that might qualify as *organizational development.*

Curriculum development may overlap with each of the preceding. In carrying out a curriculum revision, faculty members may develop additional scholarly and teaching competencies, may create new instructional materials, and may develop new communication and organizational patterns. Thus curriculum development is often an attractive vehicle for faculty development in the broadest sense.

It may be recognized that though faculty development is ultimately aimed at improving students' learning and at enhancing their education, it is likely to be but a small part of the mosaic of student educational experience. Some efforts within the faculty development movement have been directed at identifying and clarifying the ways in which students develop and learn. Attention to faculty teaching styles has its counterpart in attention to student learning styles and the fit or lack of fit between the two. Inescapably, attention to how a faculty member teaches draws attention to how students may learn. Within the faculty development movement then, faculty attention has been directed not only to learning theory but to theories about cognitive and personal development. Piaget's findings have been extended to adolescents and adults. Physical scientists have found that many college students, like Piaget's children, think only in concrete terms and lack the kinds of abstract concepts often taken for granted in science courses. Perry's (1970) description of student conceptual development moving *from* the belief that the teacher must teach the truth *to* the ability to accept complex alternative perspectives has also been useful to many faculty members.

This general describing and classifying of faculty development activities accords well with the kinds of specific activities identified by Centra (1976) in his study of over 1,000 institutions. They comprise six groups of practices: *instructional assistance, workshops and seminars, grants and travel funds, emphasis on assessment, traditional teaching practices,* and *publicity activities.*

The codifying of faculty development is not as important as getting colleges and universities to give specific attention to teaching and learning beyond that given to the scholarly accomplishments of a faculty and the courses and credit hours amassed by students. When institutions do give specific attention to faculty development, broadly considered, or to any of the categories of instructional, curriculum, or organizational development, they probably choose to concentrate on specific or limited targets or to attempt to create a broad range of effects. Thus, most faculty development programs can be roughly described as inclining to either a *single-focus* or *cafeteria* approach.

Emphases in Faculty Development

The most extensive activities within faculty development programs are those in support of individual faculty members' professional growth. Grants, fellowships, or leaves (including sabbatical leaves) are typically intended to enable faculty members to carry out research or scholarly activities that will enhance competence in their disciplines. While not excluding such direct assistance of research and scholarship from faculty development, many programs emphasize kinds of professional development that seem likely to have a positive impact on teaching. That emphasis has not drawn a sharp line between scholarly development and increased teaching competence. But it has stressed that professional growth involves an enlargement of teaching capacities fully as much as improving research productivity. Such growth may be a matter of enlarging a faculty member's knowledge of learning theory and pedagogical practices, of increasing the professor's interest in and commitment to teaching, of reinforcing and rewarding excellent teaching, and of providing opportunities to bring about this kind of growth.

A second emphasis in faculty development is that of developing additional teaching skills. One needs to have available a repertoire of teaching skills if one is to be effective for different kinds of students and different kinds of learning goals. Thus skills in planning and organizing courses, skills in using a variety of teaching methods, skills in the use of technological aids, skills in evaluation, and skills in modeling and stimulating problem solving and learning strategies are all learnable and useful if one is to develop as a faculty member. In addition, there are specific discipline-related skills in teaching, such as how to teach particular concepts or types of materials.

A third potential emphasis in faculty development is in gaining a better understanding of students. If one is to teach effectively, one must build bridges between what the teacher knows and what the student is trying to grasp. One must understand how students differ in their experiences and ways of thinking and one must also understand differences among students in motivation for learning. One must also understand the many negative influences on a student's learning—how past failure, fear, peer pressures, internal conflicts, and the like inhibit learning. No one method is equally effective for all students. If one is to be an effective teacher, one must understand students in order to provide varied opportunities adapted to differences among them.

A fourth emphasis concerns development of skills and understanding having to do with interpersonal relationships with students. The sense that a teacher cares about the student is vital to most students' learning. Research by Wilson and others (1975) and other scholars indicates that the most effective faculty members work closely with students outside of class as well as in. Many faculty members lack confidence as well as skill in developing the kinds of relationships with students that are conducive to student learning and to students modeling themselves after the faculty member. In most colleges and universities, advising is a task carried out indifferently by many faculty members. Developing better advising on the part of faculty has direct consequences for improved student learning.

A fifth emphasis in faculty development, which is not frequently considered, has the potential for promoting faculty growth. Faculty members can become better teachers by gaining greater understanding of how their disciplines' organizational structures facilitate or inhibit student learning. Simply knowing a field as a scholar is not the same as understanding its structure for teaching. One communicates differently to those who are experts in a field than to those who are novices. Attracting students to a discipline is as important as working with majors and prospective graduate students. Improving the teaching of introductory classes in most disciplines is a neglected but vital responsibility.

Sixth, motivation and enthusiasm are vital for faculty development. Other things being equal, those faculty members who are most highly motivated and most enthusiastic about teaching are likely to be most effective. Faculty development activities that enable faculty members to find greater intrinsic satisfactions in their teaching are important for continued development. Such motivation may be individually fostered, but it may importantly arise from creating a climate that inspires commitment and enthusiasm. Though faculty development programs tend to dissociate themselves from the institutional reward structure, an equitable, well-understood, and accepted reward structure is vital to extrinsic motivation.

A seventh emphasis in faculty development is that of learning how to continue learning from one's experiences as a teacher and to increase opportunities for faculty to learn from one another. The ability to analyze the teaching situation, to monitor one's own effectiveness, and to adapt one's methods to a particular class and a particular teaching situation are elements in continuing development as a faculty member.

Carried a step further, this enlarged and continuing learning on the part of an individual faculty member affects most aspects of teaching and learning. Faculty members must engage themselves in curricular development and decisions, not only within a department but within the larger college and university. Governance responsibilities that affect teaching and learning are also faculty responsibilities. All that array of duties that comprise the citizenship responsibilities of a member of an academic community have a place in this broad area of faculty development.

Finally, development in working with other faculty members, in establishing communication with colleagues who can support, critique, and assist in one's teaching—these are all important for continued learning and development. Many colleges and universities, small and large, however, currently suffer from a lack of collegiality among faculty. Whatever a faculty development program can do to open up conversation among faculty, to assert a sense of common purpose, to rally often dispirited or isolated faculty members to a commitment to teaching and learning is development of a most important kind.

Fitting Faculty Development to Faculty Needs

A faculty member may need different kinds of help at different career stages. Beginning teachers in particular need to develop the basic skills required to help classes run smoothly and reasonably effectively. Workshops on lecturing, leading discussions, constructing tests, and coordinating laboratories may help the novice avoid the kinds of errors that lead to student frustration and teacher despair. The new faculty member fresh from graduate school is usually presumed to be a competent scholar with up-to-date understanding of his or her discipline, but there may still be many needs in professional scholarly development:

1. New faculty members may be required to teach courses outside their area of specialization; for example, even an introductory course may include topics not included in a new faculty member's graduate training.
2. The new faculty member may have knowledge of theoretical developments at the forefront of the discipline but lack a clear understanding of the concepts and cognitive structures useful in building understanding at the undergraduate level.
3. New faculty members need time to deal with the expectations placed upon them. The Fink (1984) study of beginning geography teachers found that they were not only teaching large numbers of classes but also many classes requiring different preparations. In addition, many were involved in finishing dissertations, preparing articles for publication, and serving on college and university committees.
4. The new faculty member, in particular, needs a great deal of information, not only about such teaching matters as student characteristics, testing and grading practices, lecturing and discussion, and the like, but about how the institution runs. What are the sources of support and stimulation? What are library and laboratory resources, and how available are they to students?
5. As basic instruction skills are acquired and responsibilities are met, the young teacher may be particularly well served by opportunities to explore innovative ways of teaching or to work with more experienced teachers or to develop ideas about courses and teaching that may entail research and experimentation.

All of these and other needs may make the development of new faculty a distinctive part of a faculty development program. It may also make a faculty development director or committee sensitive to the situations that confront new faculty members and neither expect too much from their participation nor leave them out altogether.

What has been said in detail about the needs of new faculty members may also be set forth with respect to faculty at mid-career or as they move to retirement. No sure base of theory gives guidance here, nor are needs probably as similar and ascertainable as among new faculty. Yet there are some encouraging signs. Studies of faculty at different career stages reveal that many faculty members develop a stronger interest in teaching in the last half of their career (Blackburn and Havighurst, 1979; Maehr, 1984). At the University of Michigan, full professors are overrepresented in workshops on teaching (Smith, 1981). Opportunities to learn new skills or to adopt new approaches to teaching may attract many tenured faculty members who have the security needed to strike out in new directions.

For most faculty members, promotion to full professor comes before fifty, leaving twenty or more years of service still to come. Levinson and others (1978) have proposed that a mid-life transition occurs around the age of forty that involves an assessment of what an individual has achieved and what goals may or may not be achievable in the future. For many faculty members, achieving full professional status probably makes mid-career a period of both satisfactions and disappointments, the seeking of new directions and the closing off of old ones. Wisely conducted, the review of tenured professors may be an opportunity for the individual to not only privately review the record but to discuss further career directions with supportive peers.

Baldwin (1984) discusses the usefulness of small-grant programs targeted specifically at the forty- to sixty-year-old faculty member and the wide variety of purposes a flexible program may serve. He also endorses a change of scenery as particularly beneficial to career growth of established professors. Free from some of the pressures that fall on younger faculty, this group of faculty can both serve and be served by their being engaged in temporary administrative assignments, interdisciplinary work, development of new programs, summer internships in related but nonacademic settings, and the like. It might be of great benefit to both senior faculty members and institutions to free some of these faculty members from departments altogether and have them function on behalf of the college or university and its broader educational aims. It is also worth considering that some of this cohort will have experienced some disappointments in not having become the scholar or the teacher or the chairperson they had once hoped to become. Whatever stirring up may seem necessary to faculty members whose careers have leveled off, strong measures of support, respect, and posing of new directions are also necessary.

One of the crucial needs of faculty as they grow older is their not becoming isolated as individuals or among their age cohort. Group activities made possible under faculty development programs are important in this respect alone—bringing people of different ages, ranks, and disciplines together. Developing teaching that would rise above the merely competent needs the perspectives of both young and old. Activities that place experienced professors among younger colleagues serve not only specific aims of developing teaching competence but the general aim of keeping senior professors vitally related to the profession. At the University of California at Berkeley (Wilson, 1984) this perspective has been extended to emeriti by a program in which emeritus professors are invited to become teaching mentors for their junior colleagues.

The professional, scholarly needs of faculty members may change as faculty members lose touch with newer developments in their disciplines or assume roles requiring scholarly competence in areas that they have not previously taught. Changing conditions within the institution, discipline, or profession also have impact on faculty perception of needs. The renewal of enthusiasms in experienced teachers can be a salutary outcome of faculty development.

Perhaps in-house grants are a popular feature of many faculty development programs because they meet diverse and changing faculty needs. Such grants encourage individuals to identify both problems and opportunities and to use grant support to pursue specific individual objectives. A reasonably monitored grants program can identify cohorts of faculty attracted to or in need of specific kinds of assistance. Flexibility in grants can shift or allot funds to meet different faculty needs at different times.

Seemingly the best faculty development program would coordinate a variety of activities designed to meet individual faculty needs into a visible, attractive program that would bring faculty together in activities stimulating to teaching and effective therefore in achieving an estimable academic program. Such an ideal would be hard to realize or even to maintain in the face of the changing realities that confront most faculty and their institutions. Nevertheless, achieving some part of the possibilities for faculty growth and the expectations that students have from higher education is sufficient justification for such faculty development efforts as undertaken by the Bush Foundation in the 1980s.

❧ 2 ❧

The Bush Foundation Program: External Funding for Faculty Development

The growth of effective faculty development in the past twenty years has been largely supported by funding from external sources (Gaff, 1975). Private foundations such as the Danforth Foundation, the Lilly Endowment, the W. K. Kellogg Foundation, and the Mellon Foundation have funded programs at many colleges. In the past, both the Carnegie and Ford foundations have assisted faculty development in various ways. For the past decade, the federal government has also financed programs through the Fund for the Improvement of Postsecondary Education (FIPSE). A brief look at two major foundation programs will place the Bush regional project in a useful perspective.

The Danforth Foundation's support of higher education, now largely discontinued, had a strong personal emphasis in recognizing and supporting faculty and prospective faculty with a strong commitment to teaching. The Danforth Associate Program goes back to the late thirties and began with William Danforth's gesture of enabling some faculty members and spouses to spend a period of summer vacation at the Danforth summer home. As the program expanded, faculty members and spouses were given small annual allowances to purchase professional books and for entertaining students in their homes. Over the

21

decades, the program developed national and regional conferences to which faculty members and spouses were invited at
foundation expense. In the forty years since the program was
established formally in 1941, over 7,000 faculty in about 1,000
colleges and universities were named as Associates, a designation
honoring those faculty with a strong interest and competence in
working with students. Like the Kent Fellowships and the Har-
bison Distinguished Teaching Awards, the Danforth Associate
Program emphasized teaching by singling out individuals for recognition and support.

While the various programs did not aim at large impacts
on individual campuses, the Associate Program did consider the
possibility of creating on each campus a critical mass of faculty
committed to teaching. Experiments in this direction were in-
conclusive, perhaps because of the expense of creating such
numbers even at selected institutions and the risk of sacrificing
the broad impact of the program. For many faculty across the
country and in clusters of a dozen or more in many colleges, the
Associate Program did provide a source of recognition and reinforcement for faculty members primarily committed to teaching.

In 1974, the Lilly Endowment began a postdoctoral
teaching awards program that invited colleges and universities to
submit proposals that would introduce junior, untenured faculty to the teaching profession. Specific faculty development
programs were funded for three-year periods at various colleges
and universities. Each program funded eight to fifteen Fellows a
year; each had an identifiable director; each Fellow received released time from academic duties, frequently half time; most
Fellows worked on individual projects, and all were expected to
attend two national conferences administered by the Lilly Endowment each year. Fellows within individual campus programs
were expected to meet regularly as a group and report about
their experiences.

In a report of the program at Indiana University, Lacey
(1983) pointed to released time, opportunities to engage in consultation about teaching, being a part of the network of successful teachers both locally and nationally, and an enhanced perception of themselves as teacher/scholars as major sources of

satisfaction for the Fellows in the program. In addition, Fellows were able to identify specific instances of increased support and recognition of teaching on the Indiana campus. The most significant development was the university administration's announced commitment to a future faculty development program there.

A long-established tradition exists for outside agencies to support higher education in various ways, including explicit support for faculty. The chief condition that justifies outside support of faculty often is the absence of internal funds earmarked for specific purposes. Physical facilities and salaries place chronic heavy demands on institutional budgets of both public and private schools. Scholarships and other aids to students are always a necessity. What is left over may go into developing academic programs, providing various benefits for the faculty, and supervising and improving instruction. In most institutions, faculty responsibilities include not only an individual's teaching and scholarship but also a continuing involvement in many other matters related to instruction: developing and revising courses, examining and revising the curriculum, regulating degree requirements, instituting new programs—the list is too long to set forth here.

Usually through committee actions, these responsibilities get carried out, often with considerable grumbling on the part of faculty. Rarely do any of these activities gain a place in the line-item budget of the institution or even as clearly identified items in the college or department budget. At most, some faculty members may be given released time and clerical assistance to conduct an important study or to undertake a major curriculum overhaul. If a project is of sufficient importance, it may be carried out during the summer by faculty who are compensated for their services. In hard times, the level of such support sinks, and most of this necessary work must be carried out by faculty as part of their regular program duties or not carried out at all.

These kinds of activities are always present and in need of outside support. Moreover, they do not often fit the requirements for fellowships and grants that exist in all disciplines and that enable faculty to pursue scholarship free from teaching

duties. Research grants and fellowships carry the highest prestige and often the highest level of released time or financial support, even though there is intense competition for such awards.
Support for other activities must compete for the faculty's attention and arouse a willingness to commit time and energy to
activities that probably carry a lower priority and may mean
less to faculty members' chances of tenure and promotion. It is
probably not accidental that the recent period of increased interest in faculty development opportunities coincides with a period
of reduced research support and general financial exigency.

Supporting faculty development with outside funds raises
the question of what faculty and institutions should be expected to do for themselves. The popularity of matching grants
indicates the desirability of reaching some parity between the
institution's and an outside agency's funding efforts. With faculty development, if only because of the diversity of needs, it is
hard to ascertain which requests for outside funds are justifiable
and which are not, and what either an institution or an individual might be expected to do as part of ordinary professional
commitment and service.

The place of teaching within higher education complicates matters still further. It is a fair guess that dissatisfactions
with faculty as teachers explain in part the current faculty development movement. One indication is the very place that outside funding occupies in the movement and the emphasis such
funding has placed on teaching. That, in turn, may be because
an outside agency perceives more clearly the responsibilities colleges and universities have to students rather than to scholarship in the abstract or to the multiple demands local and national constituencies place on pluralistic institutions. Outside
agencies are also free of the pressures placed on the administra-
tions of individual institutions—to seek grants for research programs, funds for capital improvements, money for enlarging the
endowment. And as contrasted with individual faculty members' perspectives, those of outside agency personnel are not so
conditioned by academic compartmentalization, the values of
specialized research, disciplinary orientation, and building of
scholarly reputations.

A plausible conclusion is that faculty development—surely a central and institution-wide responsibility—clearly deserves internal budgetary support. Insofar as faculty development is perceived as giving greatest attention to teaching, it strengthens the case for internal support of that overarching and central responsibility. Faculty development, to be sure, cannot be narrowly defined so as to rule out a variety of competencies to be desired in a high-quality faculty capable of carrying out a college's or university's multiple purposes. Outside funding has played an important part in assisting institutions hard-pressed to support faculty even in such customary ways as providing sabbaticals, travel funds, and research grants. The greater impact, however, of outside funding for faculty development may reside in bringing institutions to incorporate in internal budgets the funding that outside agencies have provided.

Bush Faculty Development Program

The Bush Foundation Faculty Development Program came after a number of other efforts by the Foundation to assist higher education. The earliest were in the form of grants to colleges with which Archibald Granville Bush was acquainted or directly involved: Hamline, Rollins College, and the University of Chicago. Smaller grants were awarded in the late 1960s to Concordia College, Saint John's University, Gustavus Adolphus, and Augsburg College. In 1970, five separate grants were made to the University of Minnesota.

In 1972, two foundation programs emerged as a result of discussions with Minnesota college presidents, state education officials, and foundation officials elsewhere, which followed a staff analysis of trends in private higher education. That analysis recommended the Foundation's concentrating its early efforts on accredited, four-year private colleges, focusing on three types of programs designed to:

1. Stimulate recruitment of additional good students from relatively untapped sources.

2. Stimulate receipt of additional income from traditional gift sources, particularly from alumni.
3. Strengthen internal management so that colleges derive more benefit from the dollars they have.

The two programs begun in 1972 were the Bush Opportunity Grants and the Bush Alumni Challenge Grants.

The first program provided scholarships of up to $1,000 (the amount based on financial need) for graduates of Minnesota community colleges to attend four-year private colleges in Minnesota. The program paid approximately $2 million to students from 1972 to 1978 and was phased out after transfer students generally became eligible for scholarships under the Minnesota state scholarship and grant program.

The second program provided annual matching grants to private colleges to stimulate alumni giving. By the end of the 1970s, seventeen private colleges in Minnesota and the Dakotas had participated in this program, earning approximately $2.2 million in Bush matching payments and doubling both their annual receipts and the length of their alumni donor lists.

In 1976, the Bush Foundation launched essentially the same alumni challenge grants program among forty-two present and former member colleges of the United Negro College Fund (UNCF). In 1978, the Hewlett Foundation, Menlo Park, California, agreed to share the costs of expanding the program. By 1988, the UNCF alumni challenge grant program will have completed challenge grant series in thirty-one historically black colleges, will have spent approximately $3 million of Bush-Hewlett funds, and will probably achieve approximately the same percentage gains in alumni participation as were achieved in Minnesota and the Dakotas.

In addition to these two programs, the Bush Foundation's involvement in higher education includes grants to the University of Minnesota totaling over $8 million between 1973 and 1982. The largest amount of these grants went to support predoctoral fellowships in the light of withdrawal of federal support for this purpose. The Foundation tends to favor funding proposals that have university-wide or faculty-wide implications. The University of Minnesota has been the largest single institutional recipient of Bush funds.

The oldest program under Bush Foundation support, the Leadership Fellows program begun in 1965, also contributed to the Foundation's experience with motivating individuals in their careers. Though not limited to academic personnel, the program included many faculty members and administrators from the area's private and public colleges. Recipients of these awards receive financial support for between four and eighteen months of full-time mid-career study, sometimes including a specially designed internship. A number of recipients of these grants played important roles in faculty development activities on individual campuses.

Aware of conditions affecting faculty and students that promoted faculty development nationally, the Bush Foundation board began in the late seventies to think of a regional program of grants to assist public and private colleges in Minnesota and the Dakotas. One of the needs identified early was the improvement of sabbaticals so that they might be more fully utilized. An inquiry among colleges in the Foundation's immediate area of service identified other kinds of concerns. A list of possibilities included supplementary funds for research as well as for sabbaticals, support for faculty exchanges between institutions, establishment of prizes for excellent teaching and research, support of programs of peer critiquing of teaching methods and content, stimulating career change or early retirement to create new faculty openings, and assisting teachers to learn new skills and subject matters as necessitated by new knowledge and shifting patterns of course enrollments.

Various considerations began to emerge in the early planning. First, as the problem of developing faculty in a diverse group of colleges is a long-term persisting one, the program design was not to be aimed at a quick in-and-out impact. Second, an initial cost estimate of $2 million annually was set as a maximum program figure with starting expenditures considerably smaller than that. As the program has filled out, an estimated $11 million is projected to cover the maximum six-year eligibility grants in the thirty-three eligible colleges and universities.

Third, individual grants for faculty development could draw upon the Foundation's experience with alumni challenge and capital challenge grants. A balance was to be maintained between predictability of approach and flexibility in activities. Within general guidelines, institutions were to be encouraged to do careful planning and to seek planning grants from the Foundation to assist them. Fourth, plans were to come out of an individual institution's assessment of needs and best ways of meeting them. Fifth, since the aim was to improve student learning through actions of the faculty, involving the faculty in planning and proposed activities was important. Sixth, the total program needed to be such as could be administered by the present-sized Bush staff. Finally, the Foundation evinced a strong desire to keep track of what happened, to engage in internal as well as external evaluations of individual campus projects as well as of the whole Bush program. This book is the culmination of the Foundation's emphasis on learning from the experience and of disseminating the details to the academic community at large.

Developing the Bush Program

Two general approaches to administering a large faculty development program initially appeared attractive. The one would follow the example of the Bush Leadership Fellows Program and select individual recipients of grants from among the faculty of colleges in the three-state area. The other, the approach chosen, would work through individual colleges and universities, inviting each of them to submit proposals to meet specific needs and to take specific actions appropriate to that campus. A program proposal having been approved, the individual college or university would administer the funds in accordance with its plan and through an organizational structure whose activities would both aid individuals and add strength to the institution at large.

The Bush program developed its initial guidelines through an advisory committee comprised of Bush Directors Waverly G. Smith and James P. Shannon; O. Meredith Wilson, former president of the Universities of Oregon and Minnesota; Dean K. Whitla, Director, Office of Institutional Research and Evaluation, Harvard University; and Jerry G. Gaff, then Director of the Association of American Colleges' General Education Program. Looking at enrollment projections, financial prospects, faculty aging and reduced mobility, specifically in Minnesota and the Dakotas, the committee favored activities that would counter a new environment that may adversely affect the quality of teaching and the attitudes and performance of students.

From the start the emphasis was placed on improving student learning in the undergraduate college or university. The means chosen—to improve the functioning of faculty members as teachers—admittedly left a hard-to-measure gap. Could a given college demonstrate that student learning had improved over a three- or six-year period and, if so, could that improvement be attributed to the presence of the Bush program? Questions about improving the teaching performance of individual faculty members were a bit less difficult, though whether that actually resulted in enhanced student learning remained difficult to document, much less prove. In the end, this central question was resolved in a practical way. The operating assumption of formal education is that teachers and teaching count. The Foundation's hopes for student learning could rest on the positive actions of individual faculty and the collective impact of a program. A typical program would encourage many kinds of activities that had been sorted out by the faculty involved as being beneficial to teaching and learning, and subjected to further scrutiny and shaping by the Foundation staff and consultants. Colleges were asked to provide plans that recognized specific characteristics and needs of a given college. While one plan might focus upon grants to individual faculty members to develop courses, curriculum, and faculty teaching skills, another might choose to appoint a director of faculty development charged with stimulating and administering diverse activities in support of teaching.

The Bush program appeared to be manageable by a small staff, fundable to a level that could make consequential differences to large numbers of faculty and their institutions, and applicable to faculty development throughout the country. The forty-five four-year colleges and universities in the three-state area embraced a total faculty of over 9,000.

The diversity of eligible institutions necessitated a funding formula that would promote some equity among institutions. Planning in this respect also increased the common ground between the Bush Faculty Development Program and faculty development efforts elsewhere. Eligible institutions were placed in four categories based on approximate size of full-time enrollments: under 1,000; between 1,000 and 3,000; between 3,000 and 10,000 (including one state university system with seven universities within this size range); and over 15,000. As is true of institutions nationally, the smaller colleges—under 3,000 —were almost all private colleges, most with religious affiliations, although the North Dakota State College system included four colleges totaling 5,000 students. The small colleges constituted the most diverse group, including a number of nationally recognized liberal arts colleges, some well-endowed and some financially weak schools, some rural and some urban. One men's and two women's colleges were included in the group. While most offered a range of traditional majors and similar degree requirements, several offered programs outside these frameworks. The larger colleges—above 3,000—were with one exception all public institutions. While in number of colleges the small colleges outnumbered the larger by eighteen to fourteen, in numbers of students the small colleges had collective enrollments of about 45,000 while the larger had over 110,000. Both of these patterns are characteristic of colleges and college going outside the Bush program area.

Program Characteristics

Though confined to three states by Bush Foundation policy, the program included institutions representative of higher education throughout the United States. Minnesota is among the top twenty states in number of collegiate institutions and total enrollments, the Dakotas are among the smallest in these respects. Minnesota, according to the National Center for Education Statistics, has 67 higher educational institutions of all kinds and ranks sixteenth among the states in number of institutions. The state of New York has the most—298—and Nevada, Wyoming, and Delaware the least—8 in each. North Dakota, by comparison, has 19 collegiate institutions, South Dakota 20. Statistics for total enrollments closely parallel these figures. Minnesota's total enrollments of 210,700 ranks it eighteenth among the states; North Dakota and South Dakota, with enrollments of about 35,000 in each, are among the half-dozen states with the smallest numbers of students.

All the Bush-supported faculty development programs were developed locally, and with three exceptions, all were administered on local campuses by faculty offices, directors, or committees. The principal exceptions were grants made to the Minnesota State University system covering seven institutions within that system, to the North Dakota State College system embracing four colleges, and to the Dakota Writing Project jointly developed by three colleges in South Dakota and administered through Northern State College.

The size of grants supporting these programs for a three-year period ranged from $989,950 to the Minnesota State University system and $900,000 to the University of Minnesota, to $75,000 at the smallest of the private colleges. In terms of size of institutional budgets, none constituted more than 1 percent of an annual budget (at Mount Marty College) or less than 0.03 percent (at the University of Minnesota). In the small colleges, more than half the faculty participated in one way or another in the opportunities made available through the programs.

Only one of the grants, at the University of North Dakota, engaged a full-time director of faculty development provided with a fully staffed office. Most of the programs did identify a faculty development committee and part-time director, and many established a physical resource center identified with the Bush program.

Grouped according to principal type of development activity, eight colleges and universities had programs with an emphasis upon *professional growth*. These included two of the

smallest schools in the group, Dakota Wesleyan and the College
of Saint Teresa, and the largest, the University of Minnesota.
Twelve colleges and universities placed the emphasis on *instructional development.* The largest grants in this category, $375,000
and $300,000, went to the University of North Dakota and
North Dakota State University. A group of six institutions
(twelve if the seven schools within the Minnesota State University system are counted separately) chose to emphasize *curriculum change.* It need be pointed out, however, that the majority
of colleges and universities allocated funds to more than one of
these kinds of activities, in many instances to all three. Consequential *organizational change* was not a major feature of any
of the programs, though Mary College tied its proposal to its
plan to move to competency-based instruction. The academic
review component of the Minnesota State University system
grant may also be related to organizational change.

Virtually all the programs offered faculty opportunity
for grants or released time to support activities aimed at their
own professional growth or specific instructional development.
Most of the programs can be described as *cafeteria* programs
supporting a variety of individual and group activities. Those at
Carleton College, College of Saint Catherine, University of Minnesota, and Gustavus Adolphus College, and the South Dakota
Writing Project are more accurately described as *single-focus.*

Five of the programs began in the fall of 1980, thus completing their three-year cycle in 1983. All five made renewal
proposals and all were re-funded as before or in part. An additional eleven institutions completed their first cycle of grants in
1984. Six will complete their first cycle in 1985. As of July
1984, forty-one of the forty-five four-year colleges and universities in Minnesota, North Dakota, and South Dakota were included in the twenty-eight institutions or groups of institutions
who had received grants. Of these, twenty-four programs were
sufficiently under way to be included in our evaluation of progress. In the fall of 1984 the program added two colleges: Sioux
Falls College, South Dakota, and Sinte Gleska, a college chartered by the Rosebud Sioux tribe and recently accredited as a
four-year institution. The Foundation has had discussions with

other accredited colleges on Indian reservations and with community colleges in Minnesota.

Some Bush Foundation Expectations

In its announcement of the availability of grants to eligible institutions in April 1979, the Foundation emphasized local needs and local design. Applicant institutions were asked to describe their current and already planned faculty development efforts. These might include such features as sabbatical leaves, tuition programs for faculty, travel and research grants, loans, faculty exchange programs, and other counseling and career development practices.

In addition, applicant institutions were asked to project their faculty development needs six or eight years ahead to indicate how the proposed activities might meet these specific needs. How the plan was to be administered was another question, as was how the program was to be evaluated. "To what extent has the faculty been involved in designing the plan?" was a persistent question asked by the Foundation. And, as the programs went into operation, continuing questions were raised about the mechanisms and procedures established to award individual grants or to fund other activities. Strong faculty involvement in the planning and administering of campus programs was an operating principle for most of the plans.

Through these questions, two of the Foundation's important expectations were revealed. One became more identifiable as programs developed: that activities would not only have an impact on individual faculty who might receive grants but have a larger impact on the collective faculty and institutions. The other was that the institution would give administrative support and contribute financially to the faculty development effort and that plans would be made to incorporate Bush-supported activities into ongoing university operations.

The Foundation was aware both of the many faculty development needs that existed within these institutions and of the desirability of not imposing preconceptions of what comprised effective and ineffective faculty development. At the same time, Foundation staff and consultants did not accept the common notion that direct grant support of faculty along lines of their own choosing would necessarily result in improved teaching or student learning. Simply adding to the amounts available for sabbatical leaves and increasing their use seemed to beg the question. Thus, a consistent theme in the planning activities was to stress desired outcomes in improved student learning and to link support of faculty activities to these outcomes. Early in the development of the program it became apparent that a number of institutions could not respond quickly to the opportunities for funding. They needed time and resources for planning before settling on a three-year program proposal. Thus the Bush Foundation made planning grants to many institutions, and the interchange among campus administration and planning committees, Bush staff, and outside consultants did much to shape individual programs and to refine guidelines for the overall program.

Site visits by at least one member of the Bush staff and an outside consultant followed the institution's submission of a formal proposal. Though such visits were primarily to enable the Foundation to decide about funding the proposal, they also provoked further exchange of ideas that often proved useful to further planning and actual operation of grant programs. In a number of instances, site visits were made in the middle of a grant cycle. As an important part of this evaluation, another round of site visits was made as close as possible to the completion of a three-year program. In a number of instances, the same staff person and consultant made both visits, hoping to be able to note, however subjectively, some of the important changes that might have taken place.

Bush Program in Operation

With programs in place at almost all of the eligible institutions, a clear outline of the Bush Faculty Development Program now emerges. The program includes all but six of the accredited four-year colleges in the Dakotas and Minnesota and takes in the over 55,000-student University of Minnesota. The program has met needs in both private and public colleges and universities, most of which are experiencing financial difficulties. In some very hard-pressed institutions, the Bush program has been a saving presence. In many, Bush funds have made it possible to maintain faculty morale and programs necessary to minimum academic aims and standards of quality. At many institutions, the plan has enabled the college to meet new instructional needs —the use of computers, for example—and to mount and continue efforts to face serious problems—imbalances, for example, between vocational and liberal arts programs.

As common needs and problems have been identified, so certain common features of the program have emerged. One broad division is between those aspects of a program that assist individual faculty—grants, travel funds, sabbatical leave support, for instance—and those that attempt a collective impact—establishing a faculty development center, campus-wide workshops, department retreats, and other group activities. In-house grants are a feature of most programs; efforts to bring faculty together to generate activities, disseminate information, and arouse awareness and enthusiasm are also present in most programs. Finally, the diversity of the programs, which is as characteristic as their common features, arises from the involvement of faculty in shaping programs to fit the special needs and specific characteristics of an individual college or university. The total activities now going on under the Bush program probably embrace all those activities experienced within the past decade of heightened faculty development efforts.

Some Hypotheses and Observations

As the Bush Faculty Development Program went forward, the following hypotheses emerged about conditions necessary for a faculty development program to be successful:

1. That the program was likely to be more effective if members of the faculty felt that the program was *their* program rather than one imposed on them by their administration or an outside agency.

2. That an effective program required strong support from the college or university administration.
3. That programs relying to a large extent on the use and development of local expertise in leadership would be more successful than those primarily relying upon outside consultants.
4. That programs involving follow-up activities or continuing meetings of interested faculty would be more successful than those emphasizing one-shot programs.
5. That faculty members' ideas about what would best serve their individual professional development were not necessarily reliable guides to what might best serve student learning. While it might be expected that faculty would request support for released time, leaves for a variety of purposes, travel, and for revising and developing courses, more precise connections might need to be sought between faculty activities and improved student learning.

Our evaluation of the Bush program to date has, in general, confirmed these hypotheses. The first two are basic to the success of any faculty development program, keeping in mind that success often depends on a balance between faculty and administration initiatives, management, and leadership. The third is qualified by the kind and quality of both local experts and outside consultants. Confirming the fourth is difficult since it is hard to separate follow-ups and their effects from follow-up activities emerging from a successful one-shot program. Follow-up activities, however, are clearly a desirable outcome of specific faculty development efforts. The final hypothesis is related to the first two. As faculty ownership need not, and should not, preclude administrative involvement and leadership, so a faculty's ideas about what in their own development best serves student learning need not, and should not, preclude other perspectives on this complex question. A detailed discussion of these and other questions about the success of faculty development programs is reserved for the concluding chapters.

The goal of the overall evaluation of the Bush program is not to arrive at a categorical yes or no answer to questions about whether or not a particular program works or does not work. All of the proposed programs were carried out with few modifications and considerable evidence that specific goals were successfully achieved. A very few specific activities fell short of expectations. Most of the programs, however, are evolving and changing as institutions, administrative personnel, and faculty change. What this study tries to do is to determine which approaches offer promise for which purposes—recognizing that further evolution of the individual campus programs will and should occur.

One final observation is pertinent before turning to the specific descriptions and examination of the diverse institutional faculty development programs. This is to underscore the unusual care and cooperation that has gone into this project. While cooperation has been manifest among all the individuals engaged in the project and between the Foundation and the individual colleges and universities, differences in perspectives have not been masked. Individual programs as well as the overall program have probably benefited from the discussion and resolution of these differences. In sum, the details of granting, review, follow-up, and evaluation have afforded an extraordinary opportunity to ponder both the specific details as well as overall makeup of a diverse set of faculty development programs. It has also provided the opportunity to perceive these programs in the distinctive institutional contexts that do much to determine their success or failure.

❧ 3 ❧

Programs
at Private Colleges
and Universities

The eighteen private collegiate institutions participating in the Bush program are diverse in their histories and affiliations, basis of support, location, size, and even sense of mission. Most are denominational and represent the spectrum of religious affiliations in the region: Roman Catholic (seven), Lutheran (six), Baptist (one), United Methodist (two), and United Presbyterian (one). One is classified as independent though it has a denominational affiliation in its origins. Many are in small rural communities, some in small-sized population centers, and a cluster in the large Minneapolis–Saint Paul metropolitan area. With one exception their student enrollments are under 5,000, and this exception, the College of Saint Thomas in Saint Paul, only recently expanded out of the 2,000–3,000 student range. The number of faculty ranges from 41 full- and part-time at the smallest college to something over 200 full- and part-time at the largest. Most can be regarded as undergraduate liberal arts colleges, and most retain a sense of their denominational missions. Within this group, however, one finds a diversity of emphasis created by the exigencies under which many of them operate— shifting interests of students, changing relationships between education and jobs, and self-searching to examine traditional objectives and practices in light of changing conditions.

For convenience of presentation rather than from any desire to establish firm classifications, the eighteen colleges are described alphabetically within three groups based on size of student enrollments. Enrollment figures, when given, are those reported to the National Center for Educational Statistics for fall 1982 (Broyles and Fernandez, 1984). No attempt will be made here to analyze the strengths or weaknesses of these programs. That analysis is reserved for the later chapters.

When a detailed analysis of a specific college's faculty development program is provided in Part Two of this book, the reader is referred to that case study.

Six Colleges with Enrollments Under or Close to 1,000 Students

The first group of the smallest private colleges in the Bush project includes College of Saint Scholastica, College of Saint Teresa, Concordia College of Saint Paul, Dakota Wesleyan University, Mary College, and Mount Marty College. All of these are denominational colleges whose enrollments ranged from a little over 500 students to slightly more than 1,000. Although size is no precise determinant of financial stability, the smaller colleges in this group appear to be the most hard-pressed financially. The case studies of two of these colleges, Saint Teresa and Dakota Wesleyan, in Chapter Five disclose how much faculty development support can do for colleges of this kind.

The *College of Saint Scholastica,* Duluth, Minnesota, is a four-year coeducational college with 1,121 students and a faculty of 110 full-time and 25 to 30 part-time members. Students are drawn largely from Minnesota.

The faculty development program builds on previous outside support and is marked by strong faculty ownership and direction. A central faculty development committee, consisting of representatives of each of the divisions of the college, two at-large elected members, and two faculty members who serve as evaluators, administers the program. The dean is a nonvoting member.

The $177,713 three-year grant supports a combination of on-campus workshops and small grants for faculty to develop new skills, update content, and maintain professional contacts within their discipline. The program has achieved high visibility with participation of 80 to 90 percent of the faculty in one or another of its activities. The evaluation component of the program stands out for its sophistication and thoroughness.

The *College of Saint Teresa,* Winona, Minnesota, received a $75,000 grant, a substantial portion of which went to assist faculty in pursuing advanced graduate work and degrees. A detailed description of the College of Saint Teresa and its program can be found in Chapter Five.

Concordia College of Saint Paul is an accredited, coeducational liberal arts college enrolling approximately 700 students. It is affiliated with the Lutheran Church–Missouri Synod and specializes in elementary education. Its other programs are in secondary education, business administration, administration of Christian education and evangelism, and various fields of the liberal arts.

There were fifty-eight full-time faculty members at Concordia in 1981–82, roughly two thirds of whom were tenured. Forty-three percent had earned the Ph.D. degree. The addition of new staff, either from an increase in students or faculty retirements, is not likely in the decade ahead. Present faculty development support at Concordia is provided by a sabbatical leave program (three half-year leaves at half pay in 1982–83), modest travel funds, thirty-five dollars per faculty for professional society memberships, various support of divisional workshops and retreats, and some support of visiting lecturers.

The Bush grant was for $25,000 per year for a three-year period during which time the college pledged $53,000-plus annually in institutional resources. Four principal activities are supported from the grant: (1) released time for about six or seven faculty members to undertake various faculty development projects ($9,000 annually); (2) a faculty development center to assist faculty in improving teaching effectiveness ($6,500 annually for written and videotape materials and for workshops and $3,000 annually to underwrite released time for a director of the faculty development program; (3) various activities to assist faculty members in improving their effectiveness as advisers ($4,000 annually); and (4) special activities and study for four or five faculty members to improve interdisciplinary courses ($1,500 annually). The program began in October 1982.

Dakota Wesleyan University, Mitchell, South Dakota, received an initial faculty development grant of $77,400. A renewal proposal has been made for $71,250 for a program building on well-received components of the first grant and meeting some of the most important needs revealed in the first period of funding. Details about Dakota Wesleyan University and its program can be found in Chapter Five.

Mary College, Bismarck, North Dakota, was founded as a junior college in 1955 and became a four-year college in 1959. Bismarck, the state capital, is the second largest city in North Dakota; a four-year college obviously meets a need in this area. A publicly supported two-year college also exists in Bismarck, but the two major public universities are some 200 miles away.

The campus is located on the outskirts of Bismarck. The student enrollment was 1,121 in 1982, and the college has ambitious plans to increase its enrollment despite a declining pool of traditional applicants. A significant portion of its teaching faculty of fifty-two full-time members come from the Benedictine Sisters order, contributing $335,357 in instructional services in 1978.

Mary's faculty development plan is among the most ambitious in the Bush program, envisioning nothing less than transforming the faculty and program into a competency-based mode. The three-year grant of $75,000 has enabled the college to establish a faculty development center and to stock it chiefly with competency-based educational materials. A faculty development committee was established as a permanent committee in 1976–77 and administers a small number of grants that are a minor part of the program. The other means chosen to effect consequential change in the curriculum and instruction are consultants, lecturers, workshops, and faculty travel to acquaint the faculty with competency-based instruction. The major expense item is for the identification and activities of five "Master Teachers" chosen from the faculty and charged with embracing

various aspects of competency-based instruction and passing
their expertise on to other members of the faculty.

Mount Marty College, Yankton, South Dakota, is a
Catholic college with 592 students, approximately 70 percent
of whom are in nursing and allied health sciences. A large hospital adjoins the campus, which helps explain the dominance
of health-related programs. This dominance is not precisely reflected in the faculty, for of the approximately eighty full-
time faculty, forty-five to fifty appear to be engaged in administration or instruction outside the nursing and health science
programs. About half of a large number of faculty affiliates are
in health-related positions. The broad aims of the Mount Marty
program are "to preserve the integrity of its liberal arts degree
in the face of increasing accreditation pressure of professional
programs," and "to effect some change in curricula . . . to pre-
vent further erosion of those desired results of a liberal education."

Other faculty needs at Mount Marty are the familiar ones
created by low salaries, heavy teaching loads, scarce opportunities for travel and further study, and location in a small community—Yankton is 100 miles away from Sioux Falls, the largest
population center. The great majority of students and faculty
come from the immediately surrounding area. Thirty percent
of the faculty hold Ph.D. degrees, all of the degrees coming
from midwestern or Catholic universities. About half the faculty are sisters from the Sacred Heart Convent. Turnover in the
faculty is low and the faculty is relatively young.

The Bush grant at Mount Marty is for $74,900. Funds are
apportioned for a part-time faculty development coordinator
and for a development center. In addition, there are three grant
programs. One provides support of mini-grants up to $2,500
each to four faculty members annually. Another makes available training grants of $2,000 each for four full-time faculty
members to study and share with the faculty new methodologies of teaching and other aspects of faculty development. A
third set of grants, ten or so of $300 each, is for specific proj-
ects. A renewal proposal has been made along lines similar to
those set forth in the initial grant.

Six Colleges with Enrollments of 1,000–2,000 Students

Six colleges are in the group with enrollments well above 1,000 but below 2,000: Augsburg, Augustana, Carleton, Hamline, Macalester, and Saint John's. These colleges, too, are a mixed group. Included among them are some that have a national reputation and that attract students from a wide geographic area. Academic standards in some of these schools are higher than in the smaller colleges, and the ratio of students to faculty is lower. The struggle to meet financial obligations and to attract and retain students may not be as intense as among the smaller colleges, but none escapes the common problems that affect faculty morale and performance.

Augsburg College, Minneapolis, received an initial grant of $180,000 for three years with about a third going into establishing a director and general administration of the program, somewhat over a third into instructional development, and about a fifth into professional development of individual faculty. In its renewal proposal, the cafeteria approach was continued. Details of Augsburg College and its program are discussed in Chapter Six.

Augustana College, Sioux Falls, South Dakota, is a Lutheran college, whose history goes back to 1860. Located in the largest city in the state, it is the foremost private college and may benefit from being in a relatively large cosmopolitan setting.

Enrollment at Augustana has remained in the range of 1,700 for a number of years (1,968 in 1982), with roughly 50 percent of the coed student body from South Dakota, 20 percent from Minnesota, and the rest from Iowa, North Dakota, and Nebraska. The faculty numbers about 135 full-time equivalent with a projected low turnover rate in the coming years. Roughly 60 percent of the faculty have Ph.D. degrees, 30 percent M.A. degrees. Faculty and administrators reflect a well-managed, hard-working, solid academic community.

No conspicuous problems appear to underlie the Augustana program; rather it seemed to emerge from the faculty's desire for a more comprehensive faculty development program.

The $180,000 grant supports a cafeteria-type program that allots equal amounts of $70,000 to professional growth and instructional development and $40,000 to curriculum change. The internal evaluator's judgment of the initial grant period was that "activities designed to affect the faculty as a whole have been of more benefit (have had greater impact on a wider range of students) than the activities undertaken by individual faculty members."

The renewal proposal supports the same basic cafeteria program, but some additional emphasis has been placed on computer applications, interdisciplinary work, general education, and departmental growth. A substantial amount for supplemental leave support raised some questions in the face of an adverse evaluation of its range of impact by the internal evaluator.

Carleton College, Northfield, Minnesota, was awarded $92,500 in the initial grant, largely in support of a competitive program of faculty research grants ($3,000 to $6,000 each) and related activities. Carleton College and its program are discussed in detail in Chapter Seven.

Hamline University is a well-established, well-managed, and respected liberal arts college located in Saint Paul. It enrolls about 1,300 men and women students in the undergraduate college. An additional 478 attend what was once an independent law school but which merged with Hamline in 1976. The college offers the usual array of majors to a largely (80 percent) Minnesota student body. In the past decade, it has successfully attracted a large number of students (about 25 percent) as transfer students from community colleges as well as substantial numbers of part-time students.

Hamline's faculty of 87 full-time members has a strong reputation, particularly in the natural sciences and in psychology and anthropology. About three fourths of the faculty hold doctorates. The average faculty member has been at Hamline for ten years, and few changes in faculty personnel are expected over the next ten years.

A number of faculty development activities have received outside support in the past decade. A revised Bush grant proposal allotted $125,000 over three years to support specific department and interdepartmental projects, $30,000 for faculty travel and enrichment funds, and $5,000 to support departmental faculty monograph series. The sum of $20,000 was allotted to administrative costs including a part-time coordinator of a five-member Faculty Development Committee.

Macalester College, Saint Paul, and its program are discussed in Chapter Six. The college received $180,000 for a three-year period beginning in June 1982.

Saint John's University, a Benedictine college for men, has a strong academic reputation among private colleges in Minnesota. It is located in Collegeville, Minnesota, about seventy-five miles from Minneapolis–Saint Paul. Its undergraduate college enrolls approximately 1,800 men. The graduate school of theology enrolls both men and women. There is close cooperation with the College of Saint Benedict, a college for women located in nearby Saint Joseph.

Sixty-two of the 165 faculty members are members of the Order of Saint Benedict; 10 percent of the faculty is female and the recently appointed academic vice-president is a woman. The teaching mode is conservative, and faculty members are receptive to becoming acquainted with developments in discussion techniques and understanding of students that are more commonplace at other prestigious liberal arts colleges.

A one-year grant of $37,900 enabled Saint John's to begin a number of faculty development activities. A three-year grant of $179,971 followed to support activities in three groups. The first consisted of workshops varying in length from two days to two weeks in the areas of teaching faculty members skills in leading discussion, teaching writing, teaching values, and developing computer skills. Another series of activities was aimed at increasing the unity of faculty, particularly with respect to issues perceived as dividing the Benedictine from the lay faculty. A third set of programs dealt with better understanding of students, using the Perry scheme of student development. In addition, a faculty development lounge was established, and the grant supported the establishment of a faculty development library and publication of a faculty newsletter and a faculty scholarly journal.

A renewal proposal focusing on curriculum changes was funded for two years at $143,500.

Six Colleges with Enrollments of Over 2,000

The six colleges in the group with the largest enrollments are Bethel College, College of Saint Catherine, College of Saint Thomas, Concordia College at Moorhead, Gustavus Adolphus College, and Saint Olaf College. All are within the 2,000–3,000 student range with the exception of Saint Thomas where the growth in numbers of graduate and evening students has recently resulted in a total enrollment of over 5,000. The daytime undergraduate enrollment at Saint Thomas is about 3,500.

Bethel College and Seminary, located in a suburb north and west of Saint Paul, is an evangelical Christian liberal arts college owned by the Baptist General Conference. About half of its 2,069 students come from Minnesota. Degree programs in forty-three areas are offered by eighty-six full-time and eighty-three part-time faculty, 60 percent of whom have Ph.D. degrees.

The $105,500 Bush faculty development grant went for two programs, "Writing to Learn" and "Program for Excellence." The goal of the first was to involve 85 percent of the faculty over the period of the grant in teaching writing across the curriculum. The major means was a one-week summer workshop with follow-up meetings monthly throughout the year. The results exceeded expectations not only with respect to improving student and faculty writing skills but in developing greater mutual trust and collegiality among faculty members and greater emphasis upon developing analytic thinking among students.

The "Program for Excellence" proposal was supported only in part by the Bush Foundation, this part consisting of an interim term in which seven faculty members and thirty students carried out small-group projects focused on the meaning of creativity in different fields. Though faculty and students viewed it as a qualified success, the program was discontinued when funds ran out and few faculty came forward to continue it on a volunteer basis.

The *College of Saint Catherine,* Saint Paul, was founded in 1905 by the Sisters of Saint Joseph of Carondelet. With 2,285 students, Saint Catherine's is the largest Catholic women's college in the United States. Its distinctive mission, as described in the 1980–82 catalogue, is "in providing its strong liberal arts and professional programs with an explicit commitment to the educational and personal development of women." The college has 144 full-time faculty; about 25 percent are Catholic sisters, 75 percent are women. It has a chapter of Phi Beta Kappa, awarded in 1938 and the first to be established at a Catholic institution.

A planning grant assisted the college in making a broad review of the development needs of the college's faculty. The main needs identified were limited opportunities for intellectual stimulation for an aging, largely tenured faculty with high teaching loads; little time for research and curriculum revision; and insufficient college funds to support faculty research and study.

The Bush grant of $104,000 was to support a program of research and other professional development grants for the College of Saint Catherine faculty. Awards to support work during the summer ranged from $500 to $2,000 with the average close to $2,000. A maximum of twenty grants were to be awarded in any one year. Various earmarking of the grants—for example, to faculty who had not published within the past five years—was a feature of the program, as was the shaping of guidelines to favor study leading to new specializations or skills, development of interdisciplinary course offerings, adaptations of courses to changing student populations and to keeping current with developments in academic disciplines.

The *College of Saint Thomas,* Saint Paul, received a grant of $270,000, largely in support of group activities. Its program is one of the few that does not include provisions for individual faculty grants. A detailed discussion of the College of Saint Thomas and its program is found in Chapter Six.

Concordia College, Moorhead, Minnesota, was founded in 1891 as a Lutheran academy to provide education and training for Christian service and leadership. It is now a college of the

American Lutheran Church offering thirty-six major subjects, including the traditional liberal arts and prevocational work in nutrition, computer science, business administration, medical technology, recreation, physical education, and social work. While in 1960 about 60 percent of Concordia's graduates went on into public school teaching, more than half currently enter applied fields. The general aim of the college's faculty development proposal was to "focus on the roles of faculty as teachers, advisers, and models of liberal arts practices."

Student enrollment in 1982 was 2,553; the faculty numbers 150 full-time and more than 40 part-time. The Fargo-Moorhead metropolitan area is the next largest population center north of Minneapolis in these three states; the presence of North Dakota State and Moorhead State universities adds to the resources available to Concordia students and faculty.

The faculty development grant of $147,050 at Concordia builds upon considerable faculty development efforts in the past. A major part of the funds finances faculty workshops and departmental self-analyses. A unique feature bridges academia and the business world in annual conferences involving faculty, alumni, corporate executives, and representatives from other Minnesota private colleges to "strengthen teaching through a better understanding of the liberal arts." Two other faculty workshops will be sponsored at a cost of around $10,000 to improve the faculty advising process. A third allotment of funds, around $50,000 for the three-year period, will support stipends for faculty research in which Concordia students are active participants. These will be awarded competitively in the amounts of about $2,500 to four "Bush Scholars" in each year of the grant. The proposal envisions its various components serving to enhance the roles of faculty as teachers, advisers, and models of liberal arts practice.

Gustavus Adolphus College, Saint Peter, Minnesota, is a strong liberal arts college affiliated with the Lutheran Church in America. It was founded in 1862 to train pastors and teachers. It is a coeducational institution currently enrolling about 2,300 students. Students come predominantly (82 percent) from Minnesota, about half from small towns and farms and half from metropolitan areas. Measured by class rank and aptitude test scores, Gustavus Adolphus is a highly selective college in its student admissions.

The faculty numbers about 175, more than three quarters of whom hold terminal degrees in their fields. A majority of the present faculty was hired during the last twenty years, after the last thorough curriculum review. The major needs identified in applying for the Bush grant were to accelerate and increase the extent of a major curriculum revision and to provide for faculty development needs.

The $180,000 grant is one of the few in the program that focuses on the curricular change aspect of faculty development. The annual amounts are about equally distributed among support for a half-time faculty coordinator and attendant administrative expenses, released time for faculty engaged in designing or redesigning general education courses, and department planning and curriculum review retreats and external consultants. As with most of these grants, the college makes a substantial contribution to the activities, in this instance about $66,000.

Saint Olaf College, Northfield, Minnesota, was funded for $178,500 for three years by the Bush Foundation. Saint Olaf and its program are discussed in detail in Chapter Seven.

Overall Observations

These, then, are the privately supported institutions and their programs within the Bush Foundation Faculty Development Project. A number of others have been approved for grants but their programs were just beginning in the fall of 1984. While the distinction between private and publicly supported institutions is chiefly for convenience of presentation, there are a number of differences and similarities worth noting before going on to describe the public institutions and their programs.

Though these are hard financial times for institutions both public and private, hard times fall more heavily on those private schools with a limited endowment and with enrollments that struggle to surpass 500 or reach 1,000. Certain fixed costs exist whatever the size of student body, and tuition money is a vital part of current operating expenses. At the most hardpressed colleges, faculty salaries are low, faculty development programs not customary, and faculty morale is often hard to maintain. At the same time and perhaps because of just such conditions, outside funds for support of faculty have a great impact on the college's successful operation.

Many of these small, hard-pressed private colleges suffer from geographic isolation. Though some of the public colleges in the Minnesota State University system are small and in remote communities, their being part of a system helps offset some of the adverse effects. In South Dakota and North Dakota, the condition of some of the outlying state colleges may be similar to the private colleges just described. In both, a feeling of being out of the mainstream of higher education is hard to escape. For those reasons, the faculty development plans tend to stress support of travel funds, not so much for research as is true of faculty at larger institutions but more to remain a part of the larger profession or to become acquainted with instructional programs elsewhere.

Among a number of these colleges that were previously engaged in preparing teachers or ministers, some maintain an orientation more toward professional education than toward higher education disciplines. The selection of outside consultants who often seem to have a considerable short-term impact on faculty thinking also gravitates toward professional education. In some denominational institutions, the faculty includes both lay faculty and those in religious orders. In general, the proportion of lay faculty is increasing, adding to the financial problems and perhaps contributing to the reexamination of objectives and practices of the academic program. As evaluators, we were particularly interested in the ways these institutions were using the Bush grant to meet their special needs at this period in which financial and student pressures often threatened their traditional goals.

Finally, the prestigious private liberal arts colleges may have an even more difficult time than comparable public institutions in maintaining a balance between teaching and research.

The private colleges with the greatest academic reputation attract to their faculties individuals who have been shaped by the standards and values of major graduate schools. The colleges themselves tend to reflect those values; though such private liberal arts colleges place great emphasis upon teaching, they also maintain direct and indirect pressures on the faculty to be publishing scholars. Hence, almost all the faculty development proposals coming from faculty of such institutions give first priority to grants that will enable individual faculty members to maintain or establish scholarly reputations. Such pressures also exist in public institutions, particularly at major state universities heavily engaged in research. In the state colleges, the populist nature of the student body and the practical orientation of much of the constituency may put somewhat less pressure on faculty for research productivity and put more emphasis on teaching and service activities. At the same time, administrators may be trying to achieve for their departments and colleges a status that comes with published scholarship.

Other causes of similarities and differences may be as important as the form of support. Institutions of similar size, whether public or private, and with similar selectivity or lack of selectivity of students may have much in common. Differences and similarities in backgrounds will also play a part, as will location. This chapter and the ones that follow not only describe and analyze a variety of faculty development programs and activities but attempt to relate them to the characteristics of a variety of institutions. Internal comparisons that may be made among these Bush-supported programs may also be useful to similar colleges and universities considering the development needs and opportunities of their own faculties.

❧ 4 ❧

Programs
at Public Colleges
and Universities

Faculty development programs in the dozen publicly supported colleges and universities do not differ greatly from those in the private colleges. The majority of programs in public institutions, like those in the majority of private colleges, support a number of activities. A good many can be described as cafeteria programs. The University of Minnesota's program, however, is like Carleton's in that its single focus is to support individual faculty scholarship. Except for the College of Saint Thomas, all the colleges and universities with enrollments of over 3,000 students are publicly supported. At the extreme is the University of Minnesota, with over 55,000 students on one campus and approximately 4,000 faculty. The aggregate of students in the Minnesota State University system is also large—33,573 in 1980-81—but these are distributed among seven separate universities ranging from about 1,000 students (Metropolitan State) to almost 11,000 (Mankato State). A total of about 1,700 full-time equivalent faculty teach at these state universities.

The size and the diversity of large institutions create needs and problems that help shape their faculty development programs. The University of North Dakota, for example, has the only full-time director of faculty development and a fully staffed office supported by the Bush grant. The difficulties of reaching the faculty in all the colleges of a university of this size or larger may necessitate different kinds of efforts from those common to smaller institutions. As another example, the desirability of supplementing sabbatical leave funds is particularly attractive to large institutions like the University of Minnesota that emphasize research productivity and that seek forms of support available to the entire faculty.

As with the previous chapter, this one will limit itself to descriptive sketches of these individual programs. A later chapter will examine in detail a number of faculty development programs within the publicly supported institutions.

Minnesota State University System

The grant to the Minnesota State University system is the principal grant within the Bush program that is not administered by an individual institution. (The Dakota Writing Project involving three state colleges in South Dakota and a grant made to the North Dakota Board of Higher Education for four state colleges in that state are the other exceptions.) The Minnesota grant is administered from the office of the chancellor and through a general advisory committee representing faculty, administration, and middle-management staff at the seven institutions in the system. These institutions are Metropolitan State, a two-year, upper-level urban university in Minneapolis–Saint Paul, and four-year universities at Saint Cloud, Mankato, Winona, Marshall, Bemidji, and Moorhead. Faculty at all these institutions have an opportunity to participate through six activities: student/teacher research projects; Chancellor's Fellowships; curriculum development grants; residencies for visiting scholars, artists, and so on; faculty internships off campus; and the Minnesota Writing Project. In addition, academic program review is an integral part of grant-supported activities.

The Minnesota State University system operates under a ten-member State University Board appointed by the governor. The oldest of the universities now under its jurisdiction is Winona State, established in 1860 as a two-year normal school with the single purpose of educating teachers. Four others, Mankato, Saint Cloud, Moorhead, and Bemidji, have similar origins. By the 1920s these schools were expanded into four-year teachers' colleges offering bachelor of education degrees. In 1957, the legislature changed their designation from teachers' colleges to state colleges, thus recognizing their growth into comprehensive, multipurpose institutions. Master's degree programs in fields other than education were authorized in 1963. The same year, the sixth college, Southwest State of Marshall, was authorized; it began offering instruction in 1971. In 1975, all the colleges in the system were designated as state universities. The last university to be added to the system was Metropolitan State, authorized as an innovative, upper-level university in 1971. This institution, using community facilities and large numbers of successful professionals as part-time faculty, focuses on competency-based, individualized education.

The majority of faculty in the system were hired in the 1950s and 1960s. About 70 percent are tenured, and about half hold doctorates. Hiring of new faculty has declined sharply in recent years, and faculty turnover probably will not be great in the decades ahead. Teaching loads within the system are heavy, as compared with those at public and private research universities. Since 1977, faculty development has been a high-priority item. The legislature has approved between $500,000 and $650,000 per year since then for a variety of projects to improve teaching and learning. Faculty and the State University Board have operated under a collective bargaining agreement since 1975 that recognizes the Inter-Faculty Organization/ Minnesota Education Association as the exclusive faculty bargaining agent.

The grant to the system, $989,950 for three years, was the largest single Bush grant. These funds, however, served faculty at seven institutions that enrolled approximately 34,000 students: the smallest, Metropolitan State, with about 1,000 full-time students and fourteen-plus full-time resident faculty (but with a large part-time faculty); the largest, Mankato State, with almost 11,000 students and 572 faculty. The largest amount of funding, $284,700, was allotted to the Minnesota

Writing Project. Each year Chancellor's Fellowships, residencies for visiting artists and speakers, and off-campus internships were supported to the amount of $55,000 each. Curriculum development grants totaled $24,000 annually throughout the system, and student/faculty research projects were supported at about half that figure. A total of $157,500 for the three-year period was allotted to systematic review of academic programs on each campus, with the system contributing an increasing amount of the total cost of these reviews.

All these grants are administered through the chancellor's office under the direct supervision of the associate vice-chancellor for academic affairs. During the third year of the grant, fiscal and program administration was sharply decentralized. A general advisory council consists of faculty members and the academic vice-presidents of the seven institutions. Some of the campuses have faculty development committees that help disseminate information, encourage applications, and do other supportive faculty development work involving institutional as well as Bush Foundation funds. The chancellor's office publishes a newsletter informing faculty at all institutions of available opportunities, activities on individual campuses, recipients of awards, and the like.

The overall program was developed by discussion among faculty and administrators at the individual campuses and coordinated by a system-wide task force. Evaluations were conducted by individual institutions, and, in addition, an outside evaluator was engaged for the project as a whole. The various parts of the program have differing degrees of involvement overall but began at different times on different campuses. Faculty at the individual universities responded in a variety of ways to the other program opportunities available within the system's program. Some have tended to develop more proposals for certain activities than others, probably reflecting a selection to meet individual campus development needs. As the program has gone along, the number of awards received by each university roughly accords with the size of the institution. Two unique aspects of the program are support for faculty internships in business corporations and the Chancellor's Fellowships for improvement of student learning. Three Chancellor's Fellowships were awarded each year for full-time support of individuals "to delve more deeply into the pedagogy of their disciplines" and to present the results of their year's work to other campuses. (Both features were dropped in the renewal proposal.)

Bemidji State. Bemidji State was founded in 1919 to serve Minnesota's north country. A substantial number of students major in education. The university is in the middle range in size, having a full-time equivalent (FTE) of 4,196 undergraduates in 1980–81 and 208 faculty.

The Joint Professional Development Committee of the senate surveyed the faculty in 1980 and arrived at these priorities for faculty development: an improved sabbatical program, significant increases in travel funds, and greater availability of released time for research and publication. The committee also emphasized the desirability of more department funds for special projects to promote professional development, increased funding for faculty research and improvement grants, establishment of multidisciplinary workshops and seminars, and allocation of funds for faculty development consultants. As this needs assessment indicates, sabbaticals, faculty improvement and research grants, travel funds, released time, and other aids to faculty development do exist but are not considered adequate. During 1978–79, for example, $13,418 was allocated for faculty improvement grants going to thirty individuals.

The opportunities under the Bush grant have been well received. A threefold increase in applicants was experienced during the first two years. Residencies have been particularly successful, one in Canadian studies helping to strengthen a program of particular relevance to Bemidji State. Bemidji was also responsive to establishing faculty/student research teams.

Mankato State. With almost 11,000 students and 572 faculty, Mankato State is the largest university in the system. Mankato is a city of 40,000 and offers employment and cultural opportunities for its students without taking on the characteristics of a large urban setting. Because of its size, the student body is diverse, and the curriculum is broad enough to meet needs of both traditional and nontraditional students. In addition to the more than 100 majors and 50 minors offered in the six colleges, preprofessional education in medicine, law, engineering, and seven other areas is available. The master of arts, master of science, and master of fine arts in theater are offered.

The Faculty Improvement Committee has been in place at Mankato for about ten years. In addition, customary forms of faculty development support exist here as at other universities in the system. Faculty improvement and research grants go to between fifty-five and sixty-five faculty annually. About twenty-five faculty are eligible for sabbatical leaves each year. These provide a full year at half salary, two quarters at two thirds, or a quarter at full pay. Priorities in new directions for faculty development are establishing and maintaining five-year academic program reviews (included in the system grant), improving the educational experience of entering freshmen, and developing service and applied research for the region.

Two faculty members at Mankato State served as interns to major business concerns in 1982–83. A month-long residency of the Delphi String Quartet scheduled through the academic year was a highly praised addition to the academic program and enjoyed as well by members of the community. The development of the Valley Writing Project as an expansion of the Minnesota Writing Project funded under the system grant involved the largest number of faculty and was recognized as having great potential both for improving writing and as a tool for faculty renewal.

Metropolitan State. Metropolitan State is unique among the state universities and one of a handful of similar institutions nationally. It was established by the legislature in 1971 chiefly to serve adult residents of Minneapolis–Saint Paul who had completed part of a four-year program. Instead of choosing conventional majors and minors, students are assisted in designing individual degree programs to fit with past experience and future aims. Of the approximately 2,000 students enrolled each quarter, nearly 30 percent of the graduates go on to pursue graduate degrees.

Just as Metropolitan does not have a conventional campus but uses community facilities, so its faculty is composed of a small number of resident full-time faculty and a large number of part-time community faculty, professionals employed full-time in their various fields. Student learning is not confined to formal class work but includes internships, independent study, tutorials, and on-the-job training. A narrative transcript focusing on the development of competencies is provided to students rather than credits and grades.

Faculty development efforts and needs at Metropolitan are obviously different from those at other universities in the system. In the past, Metro has participated in activities of the Danforth-funded Center for Individualized Education and of the Council for Advancement of Experiential Learning. Each year Metropolitan holds five to seven half- or full-day teaching skills workshops for full-time resident and part-time faculty.

A survey of resident faculty in 1979 identified serving the diversity and needs of faculty and staff and capitalizing on Metropolitan's experience with individualized education programs for adults as future directions for faculty development. The survey also emphasized the faculty's desire for a greater institutional commitment to professional development.

Within the Bush grant activities, the awarding of Chancellor's Fellowships to three Metropolitan State faculty in successive years has had greatest impact. Not only have these fellowships had the specific impact arising from the individual's activities—one fellowship supported the development of teaching seminars for faculty in the humanities—but the general impact of conferring professional recognition on a largely part-time faculty.

Moorhead State. Moorhead State, with about 5,500 students and 260 faculty, has similar programs to those at the other medium-sized state universities. Its location on the northwestern boundary of the system, in the Fargo-Moorhead urban (120,000 population) area, and in a community with two other colleges, makes it different in a number of ways. Though most of its students are drawn from Minnesota and North Dakota, it prides itself on attracting students from all fifty states and many foreign countries.

The presence of Concordia College in Moorhead and

North Dakota State in Fargo supports a tri-college arrangement whereby students can take courses, work on degree programs, and use the libraries of each institution. The size of the two-city metropolitan area offers cultural attractions, recreational activities, and job opportunities attractive to both students and faculty.

Moorhead State was the originator of the Minnesota Writing Project, that part of the Bush system-wide grant receiving the largest funding and having the greatest impact. Modeled on the University of California Berkeley/Bay Area Writing Project, the concept was introduced at Moorhead by an English department faculty member, Keith Tandy, who had observed the Bay Area Project while completing his doctorate at Berkeley. He organized the Prairie Writing Project for Moorhead faculty in cooperation with North Dakota State and Concordia College. Grants previous to that of the Bush Foundation helped extend the project to some of the other state universities. Under the Bush grant, writing projects have been established at all the state universities.

Like faculty in the system's other universities, Moorhead's faculty is primarily a teaching faculty. The ratio of students to faculty is high—twenty-three to one—and the customary teaching load is thirty-six quarter credit hours per year, or three to four classes per quarter. Nevertheless, faculty members identify strongly with their disciplines and are concerned with achieving professional recognition despite a lesser level of support for such activities than most would like.

Saint Cloud State. Saint Cloud State is the second largest institution in the state system, with a student enrollment of around 10,000 and a faculty of approximately 500. Like Mankato State, its degree programs include master's degrees in a number of areas. Four-year degree programs not offered by other universities in the system are in arts administration, biomedical science, industrial engineering technology, insurance and real estate, Latin American studies, nuclear medical technology, photographic engineering technology, and quantitative methods and information systems. An emphasis on international understanding is related to residential undergraduate study programs in Denmark, England, France, Germany, and Spain.

Through the years Saint Cloud has supported, as have the other universities, a variety of faculty development opportunities, including modest provisions for sabbatical leaves, faculty travel, and released time or leaves for research and other professional activities. An unusual opportunity is support for about fourteen faculty annually to take teaching and administrative assignments in the overseas program. Faculty response has come up to the expectations of the administration, though both faculty and administrators speak of the need for greater recognition of faculty and institutional achievements.

In writing of future faculty development directions, the vice-president for academic affairs placed emphasis upon integrating individual faculty projects with the missions of the university. "These missions are broad and encourage pure research, wide areas of service, and all manner of approaches to better teaching."

Perhaps because of the size of its faculty, Saint Cloud has participated in most of the opportunities afforded by the Bush grant. A Chancellor's Fellowship has greatly assisted the university in its emphasis on international education. The Minnesota Writing Project has been established and extended on the Saint Cloud campus. Saint Cloud also provided an early successful model of program review in the state university system.

Southwest State. Southwest State in Marshall is one of the newest and smallest of the state universities. Located in a rural area, it was established in 1963 to provide liberal arts and technical-vocational programs. Probably more than the other schools in the system, it is a regional university, with its program of studies of rural America a defining feature. The usual array of majors and minors is offered with an emphasis upon career education. Forty percent of its students take business majors.

Southwest has an enrollment of about 1,500 students and a faculty of about 100. Faculty of Southwest may feel more isolated than do faculty at any other state university. The newly built campus, however, is an attraction in itself, and its hotel, restaurant, and institutional management programs have a strong attraction for career-minded students.

Since the university was only established in 1971, the faculty at Southwest is relatively young. The majority began their teaching careers at Southwest and have continued on, weathering severe periods of retrenchment and some administrative turnover. Faculty development has not been strongly established as a concept in which administration and faculty would be cooperatively and effectively engaged. All means by which faculty could have stronger ties with other universities and other faculty have high priority at Southwest.

Being associated with the system-wide project has assisted Southwest in the general way of creating an awareness of opportunities now available to state university faculty. Faculty participation has not been large, however, perhaps because the faculty has not previously experienced, as have most faculty at other state universities, the presence of specific faculty development activities.

Winona State. Winona State University is one of the three middle-sized (about 4,000 students and 200 faculty) universities in the system. Its roots are in teacher education, going back to its normal school origins in 1860. In addition to its customary degree programs and majors, it has an accredited nursing program and offers a master's degree in business administration.

Winona's faculty is very much a teaching faculty, and the university cooperates academically, socially, and culturally with two private colleges: College of Saint Teresa and Saint Mary's College. Winona is a city of about 30,000 and offers an attractive setting for students, most of whom come from Minnesota and Wisconsin.

Faculty development at Winona has had the opportunities—sabbaticals, professional improvement and research grants, travel funds, and released time—available to other universities in the system. In addition, funds have existed in the recent past to bring artists, speakers, and cultural attractions to campus. Institutional and outside funding has also existed to support specific programs in various colleges and departments. A newly begun

Winona State Foundation also provides some funds for such faculty development purposes as faculty travel, matching funds for grants, a special library acquisition, and support of a junior honors program.

Winona State began the Great River Writing Project effort in 1980, drawing upon the Prairie Writing Project experience. Bush grant consultants were used to review a number of academic programs, and two residencies were well received.

North Dakota Board of Higher Education

Through the North Dakota Board of Higher Education, a faculty development program was begun in October 1982 at four state colleges, in Dickinson, Mayville, Minot, and Valley City. Together these institutions enroll about 5,000 students and employ 300 faculty. They offer undergraduate programs in business, education, liberal arts, and other areas. Minot State College, the largest of the four, also offers several master's degree programs. Most of these colleges began as teacher training colleges and continue to carry out that function.

These colleges have very limited faculty development opportunities. The North Dakota state legislature has provided no funds in their budgets for faculty and staff development. Each college had received federal support of about $35,000 per year under the Title III program, "Strengthening Developing Institutions," but federal support of these programs was ended in 1981.

The Bush grant of $359,950 is divided among three major components: a writing improvement project, curriculum evaluation, and a small grants program. About one fourth of the total, $82,400, goes to writing improvement, $225,000 goes to small grants, and $52,800 goes to curriculum evaluation. A central committee composed of academic officers and coordinators from each of the colleges sets statewide guidelines. Each campus operates with a local coordinator and a faculty development committee. These committees have administered small grant funds and funds for curriculum development. The writing project has attracted faculty interest on all campuses. Evaluation committees also have been established on each campus.

North Dakota State University

North Dakota State University is a representative land-grant university with about 7,300 students drawn largely from North Dakota and surrounding states. It and the University of North Dakota at Grand Forks are the leading higher educational institutions in the state. As a land-grant university, it embraces not only the colleges and general undergraduate majors offered in large universities but has colleges of agriculture, engineering and architecture, and home economics. Doctoral degrees are offered in agricultural entomology, animal science, chemistry, pharmacy, physics, and plant science. Located in the largest city in North Dakota, the university is in close proximity to both Moorhead State and Concordia, across the river in Minnesota.

The North Dakota State faculty development plan is a "comprehensive program with a variety of activities," in which grants for institutional improvements expend the largest amount of funds. Smaller amounts go to specific efforts to improve student advising, to increase faculty understanding of students and student development, to support a number of faculty colleague groups, and to monitor and provide for continuing development of the program. The original grant was for $300,000 for three years. A renewal proposal shaped by the experience of the first three-year period has been approved for $300,000 funding for an additional three years.

Previous faculty development efforts aimed at teaching improvement at North Dakota State were described in the initial proposal as "scarce and uncoordinated." Bush grant activities have been administered by the director of special projects acting as overall coordinator and six coordinators from each of the six colleges. Perhaps three fourths of the program's efforts are focused on grants, the majority of which are in direct support of teaching improvement.

The reviews of the program's activities during its first three years were extensive and positive, though like other internal evaluations, they were more descriptive of what had been going on than evaluative in a precise sense. Nevertheless, these evaluations accorded with the views of the site visitors during the third year of the program. Faculty participation was high, reaching substantially more than a majority of the faculty in its various activities. Of particular importance was the presence of various group activities that appeared to increase collegiality across the campus and to have a positive impact on faculty morale. The program appeared to be working well and provided a model for a decentralized program that still achieves results that affect the university at large.

South Dakota State Colleges

Neither North Dakota nor South Dakota has a system of state colleges or universities as extensive as the Minnesota State University system. Three South Dakota state colleges—Northern State, Black Hills State, and Dakota State—jointly developed the Dakota Writing Project, which is supported by a $175,509 Bush grant. The three colleges provide primary centers for training and development but involve other colleges and universities in South Dakota as well. The project is administered through Northern State College.

Like the Minnesota Writing Project, this writing project is modeled on the Bay Area Writing Project. Additional support has come from the Mundt Foundation and the National Endowment for the Humanities. The project chiefly works through four-week summer institutes involving college faculty members and teachers of writing in the secondary schools as well as writing workshops on college campuses involving faculty from various disciplines. Training grants for faculty are provided from Bush grant funds.

Midway in the three-year grant, about 200 teachers, half of them college faculty members, have participated in the workshops. In addition to furthering the specific aims of improving the teaching of writing among more teachers, this project has had an impact among college faculty participants of reducing a sense of isolation and effecting more communication across campus. It has also had a positive effect on the public school teachers in the project, affording an example of school/college cooperation useful in any locality.

University of Minnesota

The University of Minnesota is the largest university in the three-state area and the largest in the country if measured by total head count. Its Twin Cities campus has more than 55,000 students (almost 65,000 counting evening students), with an additional 10,500 at Crookston, Duluth, Waseca, and Morris. Total faculty numbers 4,396 full-time and 986 part-time, a greater number than the individual student enrollments of twenty of the colleges and universities receiving Bush grants. The operating budget for 1983–84 was approximately $918,000,000.

Trying to improve student learning through a faculty development program in a university of this size is difficult. Selective support of individual departments or programs is always possible and, over a period of time, may achieve a wide impact. An educational development program at the University of Minnesota was established in 1970 by the university senate to support faculty and faculty-student efforts to improve both undergraduate and graduate education. In 1980–81, $265,000 was allotted to all colleges, including those (the schools of law and medicine, for example) that do not offer undergraduate instruction. A small grants program awarded $84,000 during 1980–81 to individual faculty for course-related projects to improve undergraduate education. In addition, $160,000 was available that year for summer research leaves, and in 1979–80, about $900,000 was available in a graduate school research fund to assist both young and senior faculty. Single-quarter leaves at full pay (chiefly for research) are competitively awarded to the faculty annually. About 4 percent of tenured faculty take them, approximately 120 out of 180 applicants yearly.

Sabbatical leaves permit longer periods of work at less than full pay and are regarded by the administration as being underutilized. In 1980–81, an estimated 430 faculty were eligible for sabbaticals, and only 88 took them. A recent survey of tenured faculty indicated that one third had taken a sabbatical. Supplementing sabbatical leave support to increase their utilization is the top priority of the University of Minnesota program.

In submitting its proposal, the University of Minnesota administration pointed out some of the university's distinctive characteristics. It is a major research university of high distinction nationally; it has a relatively higher ratio of undergraduate students to graduate students than do most research-oriented major universities; it is both a land-grant institution and the only Ph.D.-granting state university in Minnesota; and it is located in a large urban area, with large numbers of students commuting. In addition, the portion of the regular faculty that is tenured has increased from about 59 percent in 1965 to about 79 percent in 1980. Thus the influence of new faculty is minimized as the average age of the faculty increases in the 1980s.

The $900,000 granted to the University of Minnesota for three years is used for augmentation of sabbatical leaves. It is designed specifically to enhance undergraduate education by asking that faculty applying for leaves describe the relationship between their research or scholarly efforts and their undergraduate teaching. The augmentation program raises the support from 50 percent of salary during a full year's leave to 80 percent. Proposals are reviewed by a thirteen-member advisory committee and submitted to the academic vice-president for approval. Funds provide for twenty-five to thirty such awards per year on a competitive basis. In the first three years, 192 applications were submitted, seventy-seven awards were made, and seventy-four were accepted.

University of North Dakota

The University of North Dakota at Grand Forks is the largest university in the state. From 1979 to 1983, enrollment at the Grand Forks campus increased from 9,505 to 11,103, with two thirds of the students coming from North Dakota, close to 16 percent from Minnesota, and the rest from other states and Canada. Something of the size of its various programs can be gained by noting that its operating budget in 1981–82 totaled close to $95 million, and its endowment fund reached over $12 million. The full-time faculty numbers about 430; just over 60 percent of the faculty hold doctoral degrees. Doctoral programs are offered in many disciplines.

Faculty development has been relatively strong in the past, with the emphasis, as might be expected, on research-related support. A director of research was established in 1976, and over $100,000 a year is available to faculty on a competitive basis for individual research projects.

The initial University of North Dakota proposal cited the specific need for a stronger program of instructional development to complement the existing programs in support of research. The initial grant was for $125,000 annually for a three-year period. The University of North Dakota is the only institution in the Bush program to conduct a national search and hire a full-time instructional development officer. The position is equal in status to that of the director of research, and both report to the vice-president of academic affairs.

In addition to support for the instructional development office, Bush funds are expended on a three-part program.

1. Developmental leave supplements are given to those faculty members who use their developmental leave to improve instruction. These supplements provide an incentive for instructional development. Up to five special supplemental grants can be given annually and can be used for project-related travel, equipment, and consultation.
2. Previous support (grants of $10,000 annually) for specific approaches to improving classroom instruction was doubled by Bush funds.
3. A new program was begun under which "contracts" are issued to applying faculty to carry out specific university-wide activities for improving learning and teaching.

The University of North Dakota program was reviewed by its internal evaluator and by Bush site visitors during its second year. The internal evaluator surveyed the entire faculty and found the program widely known and favorably received. The faculty in general believed the program had helped to improve the design of the curricula, to improve the ability of faculty members to provide high-quality instruction, and to increase faculty members' interest and involvement in change. The site visitors found the program to be a model of its kind. All aspects of the program were working, its services had become visible to the faculty in positive ways, and it had succeeded in being an advocate of teaching excellence. Administrative support is strong, and firm plans have been made to continue the program, the director's and office's expenses being brought under regular university funds, the grants and other programs to be supported by endowment funds.

A renewal proposal for the same amount as the initial one ($375,000 from July 1, 1983, to June 30, 1986) was approved. As evidence of the university's commitment, the administrative expense in the second three-year period is underwritten by the university. Some reallocation of other funds was made in order to build on strengths that became evident in the first period.

Overall Observations

Some obvious generalizations arise from these sketches of faculty development activities in publicly supported colleges. The larger size of public universities creates different problems from those at smaller, private colleges. Though there are a handful of private universities that approach the size of a large state university, the great majority of private colleges have enrollments of under 10,000 students. In most states, the majority of private colleges, like those in this three-state area, have enrollments under 5,000. In large universities like these, funds to establish campus-wide support for faculty development, or even to augment existing funds, would necessarily need to be large, as measured by what might be expected from outside agencies, though small as a percentage of an institution's budget.

The alternative of selectively supporting faculty development has been a practical one, carried out in many ways by many universities. At one campus, it may take the form of identifying weak departments or colleges and making specific budgetary allotments to strengthen them. At another, it may be in funds competitively available to departments for programs that improve the quality of their instruction. At a scattering of large universities across the country, centers for faculty development are or have been in place. The University of Michigan's Center for Research on Learning and Teaching is an example of a long-standing one largely funded by the university. During the past twenty years, centers have existed at the University of Cincinnati, University of Rhode Island, Virginia Commonwealth University, the University of Illinois, and elsewhere.

The work of these centers varies a good deal. Those most centered on developing teaching excellence across the university are probably like the one established at the University of North Dakota. Directed by an imaginative and energetic faculty member who gains the respect and confidence of the faculty, such a center can have an impact on a large university, though that impact may be harder to effect as the university size increases. The University of North Dakota is still a small university—in the range of 10,000 students—as state universities go, and what is working well there might not work on a campus of 25,000 or more.

The program at North Dakota State indicates another kind of possibility at large universities, where various common forms of faculty development support—leaves, released time, travel funds—already exist. Creating a faculty body to administer these customary forms of support and to stimulate and develop other faculty development activities may increase both the general visibility of faculty development and the numbers of faculty undertaking development activities.

The Minnesota Writing Project is still another way of creating an impact on a large campus, though the institutions embracing this program within the state system are relatively modest in size. The model this project may afford for large universities is that of targeting a basic aspect of instruction that has a significant impact campus-wide. Writing, mathematics, and use of computers are obvious targets. So might foreign languages be, or general education, or the improvement of introductory courses. The experience with the Minnesota Writing Project seems to say that participation by faculty has other desirable effects: increasing colleagueship, increasing receptivity to pedagogical matters, and arousing more attention to how students learn.

The opportunity to see how a system-wide grant works also has application to the public universities that, in many states, are administered through a centralized system. At this point, the state system grant appears to be having at least as

great an impact on individual campuses as might be expected
from separate institutional grants. The fact that most of these
state universities were formerly teachers' colleges may make
them more receptive to faculty development programs that aim
directly at improving instructional skills and strategies, course
and curriculum development, and adapting technological aids to
instruction. Teaching imposes heavy responsibilities in these
universities on faculty members in all subject matter areas. This
may make faculty members responsive to opportunities that
contribute both to their functioning as teachers and their sense
of professional status.

Within the large public universities, research productivity
is expected of most of the faculty. General conditions during
the past decade have diminished research funds even in major
public universities, and at all times such funds have been un-
evenly distributed. Recognition of the complex relationships
that exist between research and teaching is important to faculty
development within these universities, as it is to faculty of selective private liberal arts colleges and universities striving for academic excellence. Some faculty at these institutions, with their
direct connection to public support, may be under more necessity to perform a variety of service functions. Faculty development efforts may entail correspondingly varied support.

In the public as in the private colleges and universities,
faculty development programs are currently affected by anticipation of enrollment declines, continuing increases in nontraditional and perhaps less well-prepared students, and faculties
who are growing older with reduced upward or outward mobility. These realities probably color the responses of administrators of large publicly supported universities to faculty development. The numbers game, as it is played even with diminishing
numbers and scarcer resources, will continue to be played. A
faculty's willingness to take on more undergraduate students
or to enhance the education of fewer may be traded off against
continued or increased support of faculty research and the
perquisites that go with it. Given the pressures that particularly
affect faculty members of public institutions to meet commitments to research and teaching, faculty development may be
vitally important to these places in the years ahead.

Part Two

Designing and Implementing
Faculty Development
Programs:
Case Studies

The following case studies are presented here to give a close look at a diversity of institutions included in the Bush Faculty Development Program. In each study, we examine at least two institutions with some common characteristics. The College of Saint Teresa and Dakota Wesleyan University are both small colleges, located in relatively small communities, and dependent on modest financial resources. For the large number of liberal arts colleges in the 1,000 to 5,000 student range, we look closely at three colleges: Augsburg, Macalester, and Saint Thomas, all in the Minneapolis-Saint Paul area. Saint Olaf and Carleton are examples of selective liberal arts colleges that, to the convenience of the site visitors, are located in the same small Minnesota town. Finally, our examination of large public universities is of the University of Minnesota and the University of North Dakota with a briefer look at North Dakota State and the Minnesota State University system.

Our intentions are not to single out any of these colleges for special criticism or to cite their programs as models. Ob-

71

viously, much of what is set forth in these studies will be of particular interest to colleges and universities of similar kinds. Our analysis is also intended to be useful to faculty development activities wherever they may be planned or going on.

In these studies, we are interested in how the characteristics of an institution affect both the program planning and the program itself. Each study tends to single out specific problems associated with a kind of institution. Hard-pressed small colleges, for example, often need faculty development funds to support activities regarded as faculty perquisites in more affluent colleges. Colleges with highly selected student bodies may have to contend with a faculty's tendency to emphasize advancing their own research careers as the chief faculty development need. Large universities face the difficulties of finding activities that can affect a sizable portion of the faculty. The observations and conclusions in these case studies extend beyond the specific institutions and contribute importantly to our overall conclusions and recommendations about faculty development.

❧ 5 ❧

Programs at Small
Liberal Arts Colleges:
College of Saint Teresa
and Dakota Wesleyan University

The College of Saint Teresa and Dakota Wesleyan University represent in many ways the traditional American dream of liberal arts education—enrollments under 1,000, campuses in relatively small communities remote from large urban centers, and founded by, with continuing ties to, Christian denominations. Yet this dream confronts the realities of budgets that are stretched to maintain respectable faculty salaries, library, equipment, and maintenance funds; problems in maintaining enrollments in the face of declining numbers of high school graduates and increasing competition from less expensive public institutions; curricula extended to the limits to provide both a traditional liberal arts curriculum and career-relevant programs that will attract students.

Both campuses have an interesting mix of older buildings together with newer buildings constructed in the past twenty years. Both attract most of their students from the immediate geographical area and with a minority attracted by denominational or alumni ties from a wider area.

Founded in 1907, the College of Saint Teresa is a women's college with about 30 percent of its 600 students enrolled

73

in a nursing program. These nursing students are in Rochester, Minnesota, for their junior and senior years. Many of the nursing faculty members reside in Rochester and the students have their clinical placements there. Because faculty are geographically separated, it is harder to build a sense of community, and administration of the college is more complicated.

Saint Teresa shares Winona, Minnesota, with two other institutions of higher learning: Saint Mary's College and Winona State University, one of Minnesota's state universities. The three institutions cooperate in some areas, and together they have a considerable impact upon the cultural ambience of Winona. Nonetheless, faculty members need to get away occasionally if they are to maintain professional and scholarly contacts.

Roughly 60 percent of the students come from Minnesota, with the remainder mostly from Wisconsin, Iowa, and Illinois. Faculty members, too, have local ties, with many having themselves been students at Saint Teresa or neighboring institutions. Of the 63 full-time faculty members, 24 percent hold the Ph.D.; 69 percent, the M.A.; and 7 percent, the B.A. Many of those with less than the Ph.D. are nursing faculty members, and part of the Bush grant helped support work toward advanced degrees.

In contrast, Dakota Wesleyan is one of the major centers of activity in the small city of Mitchell, South Dakota. Dakota Wesleyan was founded by Methodists in 1885, four years before South Dakota gained statehood. The founders "built a college of stone, while living in houses of sod." Mitchell, South Dakota, is a city of 14,000, the home of the "Corn Palace." One of the smallest colleges in our sample, with about 500 students, the college draws its students largely from South Dakota and surrounding states and takes pride in the fact that five U.S. senators, including Senator George McGovern, have attended Dakota Wesleyan.

The college's primary mission is to offer both a liberal arts education and opportunities for career preparation. In pursuit of this mission, the college offers a variety of programs leading to a bachelor of arts or associate of arts degree. The constituency is largely rural and, in many cases, educationally disadvantaged. With a student body of only 500, one of the chronic problems of the college is to maintain that level of enrollment in a period of decline in numbers of traditional prospective students. Over 80 percent are full-time students, more than 66 percent are B.A. candidates, and 33 percent are classified as nontraditional. Eighty percent of students come from Mitchell or South Dakota. Sixty-seven percent of the students work on campus, and 88 percent receive financial aid, the estimated average aid figure being $3,600, about 50 percent of which comes from government loans. Nursing and allied health fields, church and human services, and education account for 78 percent of career preparation. Tuition, fees, and room and board are the lowest of nine similar colleges in the region. Like students everywhere, these students are job-oriented, hoping to find through their work at Dakota Wesleyan an entry into more varied and more lucrative careers than the local economy alone might provide.

Despite the pressures on probably a majority of students, the ones we talked with on both visits expressed strong satisfaction with their collegiate experience and the Dakota Wesleyan faculty. A tangible expression of their commitment to the college was the extensive refurbishing of the dormitories done largely by student labor during the period of this grant. Faculty, it appears, match this student commitment by their own commitment to the university, despite modest salaries, lack of perquisites, and faculty reassignments and cutbacks during the period of the Bush grant.

The faculty consists of thirty full-time instructors plus a number who teach part-time. The equated total is forty-three faculty. Approximately 64 percent of those eligible hold tenure. Among faculty who teach more than half time, 40 percent hold doctorates, and an additional 25 percent hold master's degrees in fields where that is typically the highest degree earned. All but two of the remainder hold master's degrees.

Faculty development is not new to either Saint Teresa or Dakota Wesleyan. Saint Teresa received grants of $225,000 from the National Science Foundation, $200,000 from the

Northwest Area Foundation and $8,000 from the Council of Independent Colleges to support a major program revision. These grants supported course development projects, in-service education, as well as other planning and learning activities. From 1978 to 1980 Dakota Wesleyan received grants of $48,150 under Title III of the federal Higher Education Act. From 1976 to 1978, the Lilly Endowment contributed $125,952. These funds helped faculty members work on advanced degrees, travel to professional meetings, purchase teaching supplies, and invite visiting scholars to the campus.

The problems of faculty development at Dakota Wesleyan and the College of Saint Teresa are conditioned by their circumstances. In both institutions, faculty salaries are modest, and neither institution is located close enough to other major cultural and intellectual centers to have special attractions for faculty members. Fewer than half the faculty members hold doctoral degrees. Moreover, both Dakota Wesleyan and Saint Teresa have had to make cutbacks in faculty in order to cope with the budgetary problems arising from difficulty in maintaining enrollments over the past few years. Both colleges had just carried out major curriculum studies with extensive revisions in requirements and course goals. Program review at Dakota Wesleyan was aimed at improving the quality of the curriculum as well as at meeting changing conditions.

These circumstances led to some similarities in faculty development programs at Dakota Wesleyan and Saint Teresa. A major part of the Bush program at both colleges involved grants to faculty members in direct support of individual faculty development—revising courses, short-term learning experiences, and travel to conventions or to find out about curricular development elsewhere.

College of Saint Teresa

The College of Saint Teresa's Bush Faculty Development Program had four major components:

1. Professional development within faculty members' own disciplines

2. Expanded exposure to other fields (interdisciplinary training)
3. Training to improve teaching
4. Training in organizational effectiveness

Specific measurable goals were established for each component, and those goals were almost all achieved; some were exceeded.

One unique feature of the Saint Teresa program was that some grants were made to give full support of faculty members' degree programs. One might ordinarily be rather skeptical about the appropriateness of such expenditures from a faculty development grant. We would usually expect that individuals would arrange for leaves and personal support for graduate education. Nonetheless, Saint Teresa's administrators argued that enabling existing faculty members to obtain credentials necessary for maintaining accreditation of the nursing program was likely to be more valuable to the institution than recruiting nursing faculty with advanced degrees who would not have long-term commitments to Saint Teresa. Many of the present nursing faculty members are alumnae of Saint Teresa or have homes in the area, so that they are more committed to permanent careers at Saint Teresa than individuals recruited in a national search.

The committees administering the program view extensive support of graduate training as a temporary expedient and have moved from full to partial support and to a wider variety of short-term learning experiences rather than continuing expenditures for full support of faculty degree programs. Participants report that being able to carry new learning from one's own educational experiences into one's teaching has motivational and cognitive value for both faculty members and students. Seventeen faculty members participated in formal credit or noncredit courses with Bush grant support.

The second major area—exposure to other fields—was an exception among the Minnesota institutions even though it represents a mode of faculty development that has been discussed a great deal in the past few years. In this case, a professor of political science who had insufficient enrollments in political science to support full-time teaching was given a grant to spend time at the Wharton School of the University of Pennsylvania to study business law, which he now teaches on campus. Investment in the faculty member's training resulted in saving the cost of hiring a local lawyer for part-time teaching. Another faculty member was given support for training in early childhood education to enable her to teach courses in this area in addition to those she had previously been qualified to teach.

The workshop program involved workshops in the use of videotapes, use of computers, and the use of information about learning styles in teaching. These workshops were attended by all faculty members, and the workshop on learning styles was described by one of our respondents as "the most productive and challenging learning experience of the past ten years." One evidence of success was that a learning styles group continued to meet after the workshop. A number of the faculty are now acquainted with the Perry theory of student development. Developing concepts that encourage communication about student learning is important not only in facilitating mutual support for teaching, but also for its heuristic value in promoting new insights to be shared. This workshop was also timely in that a major program revision had been carried out in 1979, and the workshop helped conceptualize the changes needed in course revision and teaching.

As one of the few Bush programs proposing to carry out specific organizational development activities, Saint Teresa was of particular interest to us, even though the proposed organizational development activities were generally not carried out. At Saint Teresa the college faculty governance system structure had been reorganized, and changes in hiring, promotion, and tenure policies were made that resulted in the president's request that some aspects of the original plans be omitted. Nonetheless, twenty to thirty faculty members attended a workshop on organizational theory, and ten department chairs attended a workshop on department chairing.

The reorganization of the governance structure had implications for the administration of the program. The Bush grant had been administered by a different faculty committee each year, with some movement from little to greater faculty control. At the time of our visit, the dean was chairing the Faculty

Effectiveness Committee, but the committee itself had not built up a reservoir of expertise.

The overall impact of the faculty development program seems to have been favorable. Student retention rose from 65 percent to 85 percent, and student ratings of faculty teaching competence rose slightly. These are probably signs of a general rise in morale, and faculty and administrators speak feelingly of the contribution made by the Bush grant.

Dakota Wesleyan University

Recent events at Dakota Wesleyan during the period of the first Bush grant dramatize the rapid and adverse changes that can crucially affect small colleges. When the proposal for the initial grant was made, Dakota Wesleyan was beginning to feel with increasing severity the pressure of financial exigency and declining enrollments. The college, during the presidency of Donald E. Messer, had maintained balanced budgets for eight years. In 1982, the college experienced a small operating deficit of $11,000. Concern with program quality and mounting financial pressure led to a decision in 1983 to redirect seven full-time-equivalent faculty positions over a three-year period. By so doing, it was felt that the faculty-student ratio could be decreased from one to ten to one to fifteen, a much more economically feasible ratio. Understandably, a faculty teaching a large number of classes (if not large-sized classes) and often required to develop competencies and teach courses outside their customary disciplines found the proposed cutbacks threatening. Only two faculty members, however, were laid off; the others were placed in combined faculty/staff/administrative positions.

As the administrative official primarily responsible for the grant and also heavily engaged in working out ways of trimming the faculty, the dean was placed in a very difficult position. Despite extra administrative responsibilities placed upon her and her position with respect to faculty reduction, she continued to provide necessary leadership in faculty development. In a small college, both administrative and faculty leadership can be stretched thin. Yet the job gets done and often done well.

In addition, during the first year of the initial Bush grant, a new president had come to the college full of energy, working hard to put the college on a solid financial basis. His primary task was that of building a wide base of alumni, business, and community support. He is maintaining communication with the faculty to give them a sense of the importance of this support and of his optimism for the future of the college. Nonetheless, his endorsement of program redirection and future initiatives of the college add to faculty anxiety related to change. In the opinion of one of the site visitors during the last year of the initial grant, "the general salutary effects of the Bush grant were somewhat diminished or displaced by the concern with financial exigencies felt by both the administration and faculty."

As to the grant itself, four types of activities were initially funded. They were designed to accomplish the following:

1. Assist faculty in assimilating new concepts of general education into their courses and instructional formats.
2. a. Provide opportunities for retraining of faculty to meet expanded teaching needs of the university, for example, training a sociologist in computers or training nurses in another specialty, such as obstetrics.
    b. Provide assistance in development of skills that will involve faculty (according to their interest and abilities) in activities that support the total university functions, for example, marketing, admissions, recruiting, public relations, retention, development, or program development.
3. a. Provide support for faculty to be involved in curriculum or course revision and design, for example, developing an audiotutorial program.
    b. Provide assistance in developing understandings of new possibilities and thrusts such as adult and continuing education. Workshops on adult learning were held.
4. Provide opportunities for faculty to be involved in research and scholarly pursuits.

Thirty-two of the forty-three faculty members at Dakota Wesleyan received grants for one or more of these activities, and all faculty members were involved in some aspect of the program. The grants went for a variety of projects ranging from preparation of a faculty handbook through course revisions to studio work on original seriography for an exhibit. Of the twenty-four recipients who returned questionnaires about their grants, twenty-two felt better prepared for teaching. Four reported greater involvement in the general education program; eight reported that materials purchased had enhanced their teaching. The general education program had been developed prior to the Bush grant, but a number of the faculty grants under the Bush program were made for development and revision of general education courses, an activity that was rated as highly productive by most of our questionnaire respondents. Students in the courses in the new general education program rated the courses as achieving general education goals.

Among the respondents to our questionnaire, all except one reported changes in teaching as a result of involvement in course development activities, faculty workshops, or research activity. The one respondent reporting no change had attended a lecture by an outside consultant and found the lecture to be interesting but to have little lasting impact.

The emphasis upon small, individual grants to faculty members has been useful in maintaining the morale and commitment of the large number of faculty members who have made, and are making, careers at Dakota Wesleyan. Many have a strong identification with the college. While the Bush grant has had an important effect upon the sense of collegiality by supporting special dinners and workshops, faculty members spoke of the need for additional ways of developing greater cohesiveness and sense of group support.

The success of the Dakota Wesleyan program even in the face of adverse circumstances was sufficient to gain approval of a renewal proposal for an additional three years. Dakota Wesleyan will continue with curriculum revisions, develop a peer evaluation system for the faculty, train faculty in computer use, redesign the cocurricular program of the university to improve student learning outside the classroom, and revise the faculty committee and governance structure. Aside from administrative expenses for a one quarter-time faculty development coordinator and a half-time faculty development secretary, the greater part of the funds will go to grants to individuals and teams engaged in the specific objectives of the program.

The college has mounted an ambitious fund drive in which $1,145,000 has been proposed for institutional operating expenses including quality teaching and curriculum development. In the past, from 1975 to 1979, the college successfully completed a Bush Foundation Alumni Challenge Grant program, receiving $101,000 from the Foundation and tripling the amount of annual gifts from alumni. Currently, the university commits $44,700 annually to faculty development.

Like activities within the faculty development program itself, the various efforts to gain a wider base of support for the college and the faculty development activities may work together. It is observable in this faculty development program and probably true of those in similar small colleges that specific expenditures probably have more than specific impacts. That is, in this instance, the grants given to faculty specifically for course revisions probably have the added impact of tangible recognition and support for one kind of necessary academic work. Similarly, though teams may be brought together for the specific purpose of examining general education courses, the individuals may benefit from the general opportunity to exchange educational views with colleagues. A travel grant may be the means of acquainting the faculty with teaching practices elsewhere but also add to the individual's sense of wider colleagueship and carry over to students, who benefit from a faculty member's wider experience. In a small college, the involvement of some faculty members in the administrative responsibilities necessary to carrying out a successful faculty development program may develop leadership abilities necessary to the university in other ways.

Overall Observations

The Bush Faculty Development Program grants to Dakota Wesleyan and Saint Teresa seem in many ways to have been the most critical for the future of the institutions of any of the grants made by the Foundation. Larger, more affluent institutions are less likely to have the really critical needs found in these institutions, and while one could not literally say that the Bush grant had life-or-death implications, in both institutions the site visitors felt that the grants had played a critical role in maintaining hope and enthusiasm at a time in which anxiety was realistically rife.

For example, sending members to national conventions might ordinarily be considered to be the sort of activity that should be funded out of the regular university budget, but again when institutions are operating as close to the line as these two, the opportunity to attend a national convention may be a very critical factor in maintaining faculty morale and enthusiasm. In both institutions, the faculty committees making the grants developed rigorous criteria and often gave very modest support. One of the most interesting accounts of probable impact on students came from a Saint Teresa faculty member who had had a grant to partially support the expenses for a trip to a national convention in San Antonio, Texas. She used the money to rent a van in which she and eight students drove, without an overnight stop, from Minnesota to Texas. The students had the excitement of seeing and talking to scholars who had been cited in their textbooks. En route home, the group visited a nun of their order who had been imprisoned for peace activities. After listening to the faculty member describe this experience, we would find it hard to deny the positive impact of this relatively small expenditure of the Bush Foundation grant.

These two grants also illustrate some of the problems of faculty development programs in very small institutions. Small colleges have limited administrative resources and faculty members have heavy responsibilities, which make it difficult to develop the kind of programmatic thinking and planning that one may find when greater marginal resources are available. It may also be true that mixing largely administrative needs—peer evaluation of faculty, affecting the cocurricular program, and revising the governance structure—with needs more sharply related to faculty members' professional growth draws the program away from the central aim of improving learning. But in a small college, the relationships of administrative functioning and teaching and student learning may be closer, and therefore harder to separate, than in large institutions. While neither college was able to provide strong evaluative data on the effects of their programs on student learning, this was also true of institutions with much greater resources, and both Saint Teresa and Dakota Wesleyan did carry through their evaluation plans, meeting their goals in faculty participation in the activities planned and in faculty satisfaction. Saint Teresa set measurable goals in terms of numbers of faculty completing advanced degrees, attendance at workshops, the design of computer literacy components of courses, and other teaching changes. Most of these goals were met or exceeded. Student ratings of courses were also obtained. Dakota Wesleyan obtained evaluations of newly developed general education courses from a faculty committee, from students, and from the courses' instructors. Students rated the courses particularly highly in using analytical and creative thinking in relation to the subject matter. In both colleges, individual grantees submitted products or reports of the work funded. Both colleges were more successful than most larger colleges in getting such reports. In addition, Dakota Wesleyan gave a questionnaire to all grant recipients. Responses were generally positive.

The most positive aspect of our visits to these colleges was the sense that relatively small, nonaffluent colleges have faculty members and administrators who are committed, resourceful, and dedicated to offering a good undergraduate education to the students who attend their institutions. The grants have had a direct impact on a large proportion of the faculty. Even though the amounts of money are small, one has the sense that the grants really do result in maintaining and rejuvenating the commitment of the older faculty and nurturing sparks of enthusiasm among the younger faculty.

As discussed in the following chapter, grants to faculty members were also an important aspect of the Bush Faculty Development Program at Carleton College and were part of the program at Saint Olaf College. At Carleton and Saint Olaf the grants played quite a different role, having much greater impact upon the faculty members' research and scholarly activities and less apparent direct impact upon faculty members' teaching. At

Dakota Wesleyan and Saint Teresa, highly specialized research is much less common than at Saint Olaf or Carleton, and scholarly activities are seen as playing a less central part in the academic roles of faculty. At Saint Teresa and Dakota Wesleyan, scholarship is much more perceived as involving keeping up with new developments in one's field so that one's teaching can adequately represent one's discipline.

Applications to Other Small Colleges

The others in the group of small, liberal arts, denominational colleges receiving Bush faculty development grants were the College of Saint Scholastica, Concordia College of Saint Paul, Mount Marty College, and Mary College. Mount Marty and Concordia College of Saint Paul have enrollments in the 500 range and may be most closely compared with Dakota Wesleyan and Saint Teresa. For Mount Marty, a further point of comparison is its location in a relatively small community. Neither the college nor the community has the resources to be found in larger institutions and communities. These limitations are financial—low student enrollments do not generate the income upon which these colleges greatly depend, and the smallness of the community limits adult education as another important source of income—but they affect faculty development in other ways. Internally, the small faculty may not have, at any point in time, sources of leadership necessary to a successful program. Hardpressed as faculty are likely to be, the collective faculty may not be able to generate or sustain a program. (Some evidence of these effects may reside in the quality of proposals coming from some other small private colleges, several of which were not approved for funding.) At the same time, a small college in a small community may be more vital to that community than larger colleges in larger locations. No visitor to such colleges can remain unaware of how much the college contributes to the social and cultural life of their communities. As an economic resource, Dakota Wesleyan, for example, with 118 employees, can reasonably claim to generate more than 200 jobs and have an economic impact of more than $7 million in Mitchell, South Dakota.

With regard to providing outside support for faculty development, small-sized institutions may have an attractive aspect. It was the general consensus of staff and consultants that at these small colleges, the visible returns were great for the amount of money invested. With faculties of thirty to fifty, it is not only possible but likely that virtually every faculty member's performance will be affected by faculty development activities. Given the difficulties confronting the faculty, the impact may be more than that of modest improvements here and there in aspects of the academic program. The impact may actually "renew" a faculty; a faculty development program may be a saving presence in the hardest of times.

Mount Marty College in Yankton, South Dakota, shares with Saint Teresa the effects of being somewhat dominated by a single emphasis in the academic program. At Mount Marty, 70 percent of the recent graduating seniors majored in nursing and allied health sciences. (It should be observed that the presence of a large hospital adjoining the campus at Mount Marty makes for greater integration of the nursing faculty and students with the rest of the college than at Saint Teresa.) When the market strongly shifts students into career programs, whether they are in health sciences, as with these instances, or in business or computers, to name two other attractive career options, the small colleges face serious problems of imbalance. Faculties of these institutions develop over longer periods of time; like faculties everywhere, average age and length of service has increased in the last decade. That collection of diverse faculty necessary to a liberal arts program cannot easily be retrained, even if it were advisable, to meet imbalances created by marked swings in student preferences or career opportunities. Meeting these conditions wisely and with maximal faculty involvement may be an added benefit of faculty development at such institutions as Mount Marty and Saint Teresa, in particular, but at Dakota Wesleyan and Concordia of Saint Paul as well.

Saint Scholastica and Mary College can fairly be differentiated somewhat from the colleges just discussed. Both have enrollments at or exceeding 1,000 students, and both are in communities that are both larger and more central to a region. As the major four-year institution in Bismarck, North Dakota, the state capital, Mary College has the population base for continued development. Its movement from a junior college to a four-year college and projections to expand into graduate offerings describe a growing institution. Saint Scholastica has a somewhat similar situation as a leading private college in Duluth, the largest population center north of the Twin Cities. We are not implying that faculty development efforts at the four smaller colleges are less advisable or less successful than those at the two larger institutions, with approximately double the student enrollments. Indeed, they may be both more necessary and more cost-effective at the very small college. It is probably fair to observe, however, that at the larger colleges, there may be more, and more diverse, resources among both faculty and administration that can go into faculty development. While the programs at Dakota Wesleyan, Saint Teresa, and Mount Marty are in part responses to pressing immediate needs, those at Saint Scholastica and Mary College seem to be less driven by necessity. The program at Saint Scholastica has strong faculty ownership and direction that speaks of sufficient faculty resources to be profitably channeled into development commitments that affect 80 to 90 percent of the faculty. Mary College's program is one of the most ambitious in its effort to change over an entire faculty and program to a competency-based mode.

The differences being discussed here should not distort the fact that faculty development programs at these institutions have many common features. Almost all provide funds for a combination of on-campus workshops and small grants to individual faculty to develop new skills, update content, and maintain professional contact within their disciplines. Such features obviously arise from the fact that institutional funds are not readily available for such purposes. In most of these colleges, these activities dovetail with efforts to make necessary revisions in courses and curricula.

Both Mount Marty and Mary College have placed special emphasis upon developing key faculty members to act as consultants to the other faculty members, a strategy also used at Saint Teresa. In the case of Mount Marty, four faculty members were trained to become expert in computers, evaluation, interdisciplinary courses, and improving instruction. At Mary College, master teachers were trained to induct other members of the faculty into a competency-based approach to education. The notion of developing local expertise is an appealing one, but the problem is in persuading other faculty members to utilize the expertise once it has been developed. In large as well as small colleges, we found less use of master teachers, or faculty experts, than we would have expected. It is not that prophets are completely without honor in their own country so much as the lack of urgency about using a resource that will continue to be available in the future. With an outside expert, there is "now-or-never" pressure to attend a workshop or seminar. When colleagues' workshops conflict with other demands on time, it is easy to rationalize, "I'll talk to them later." Probably the outstanding exception to this generalization was the computer workshops offered at Mount Marty. As we saw in comparisons of the Bush programs with faculty development programs in Iowa colleges, almost everyone wants to learn about computers, and one cannot pick up computer expertise in conversation over coffee.

Conclusions

Even though one might doubt the wisdom in investing in colleges with minimal financial and human resources to plan, administer, and evaluate a faculty development program, faculty development programs at these small colleges produced impressive results both for faculty morale and, most probably, for teaching effectiveness.

Faculty development funds at small, hard-pressed colleges are vital in affording individual faculty small grants to meet various professional needs. One need is that of carrying out specific teaching-related tasks that would otherwise come on top of heavy expectations as to student advising, committee work, and meeting numbers and variety of classes. Another is to maintain professional contact, acquaintance with scholarship and teaching, outside the confines of the institution. Still another is to offset the financial pressures that turn faculty members to gainful summer employment rather than to activities promoting professional growth.

Though faculty development programs at these small colleges (and through the range of colleges and universities in the Bush project) have much in common, differences in needs, objectives, and mode of operation are also present. Where institutions are hardest pressed, faculty development activities may be affected by an institution's efforts toward survival. Direct support of advanced degree work or of retraining in a different area of competence may be a feature of such programs, as may also be concerted efforts to reshape a curriculum or to affect an institution's ability to attract and retain students. At more secure institutions, programs may be more varied in seeking out ways of motivating faculty or may single out some one aspect of faculty performance for strengthening.

In small institutions of this sort, one expects to find a strong sense of community; yet the work load and demands of meeting the varied needs of the institution with a minimal staff mean that all too many faculty members, even though strongly identified with the institution, have fewer opportunities to support one another's intellectual and teaching interests than might be expected. The Bush Faculty Development Program has been helpful in this aspect of academic life, which faculty members in these institutions speak of with some sense of unfulfilled expectations.

❧ 6 ❧

Programs at Medium-Sized Liberal Arts Colleges: Augsburg College, College of Saint Thomas, and Macalester College

Pressing needs shape faculty development programs at the very small and often hard-pressed private colleges. Colleges whose enrollments exceed 1,000 vary greatly as to financial strength, but most within the Bush project built their programs on previous efforts (often funded by outside sources) and in relation to existing faculty development support. Like other institutions, however, all faced problems associated with potential loss of enrollments, shifting of student interests, and changes within the institution itself. Three of the private colleges in the 1,000 to 5,000 student enrollment range provide an opportunity to reflect on commonalities and differences in development programs, what seems to work well and why, on these and perhaps on similar campuses.

Augsburg College

Augsburg College is a Lutheran college, its present identity arriving with the merger in 1963 of the Lutheran Free Church (its founder) and the American Lutheran Church. Its roots go back to the same period of post–Civil War founding of denominational colleges as brought Saint Thomas and Macalester into being. Its move to Minneapolis in 1872 placed it in a now more urban, inner-city location than the present sites of the two other colleges. Its heritage and present condition are described as "pietistic, anti-elitist, and democratic."

Like the other two colleges, Augsburg's enrollment of about 1,500 students is largely from the Twin Cities, but with a larger proportion of middle- and low-income students. The faculty numbers just over 100 of full-time equivalent; about one third of the faculty are part-time. (Saint Thomas also relies on numbers of part-time faculty; Macalester, less so.)

Of the three colleges, Augsburg is currently under most financial strain, a fact consistent with its history. The absence of support for conventional means of faculty growth coupled with heavy teaching loads does much to explain the *cafeteria* aspect of Augsburg's plan. A variety of activities, both of group and individual kinds, are being undertaken. An annual workshop on improving teaching, other teaching workshops, stipends for course development, programs aimed at increasing computer knowledge of the faculty, improved advising, and placing faculty as interns in industry, government, or elsewhere are parts of the instructional improvement category. Most of these activities involve direct aspects of improving teaching competence. The second category is described as professional growth and supports limited numbers of summer research grants, a faculty lecture series, a proposal writing program, a department chairperson leadership effort, and similar individually oriented programs.

College of Saint Thomas

The College of Saint Thomas as a Catholic, diocesan college offering a value-oriented education to a wide variety of students. Unlike the majority of small private colleges today, it has increased enrollments dramatically since 1973, rising from about 2,400 students to a total of over 5,000 today. Full-time undergraduate enrollment, however, is slightly over 3,000 students in 1984. Saint Thomas's change in size has been marked by its adding a graduate program in business management in 1974 and becoming coeducational in 1977. There are 159 full-time teaching faculty, with a ratio of undergraduate students to faculty of twenty to one. Two thirds hold Ph.D. degrees, and 30 percent M.A.s.

The increase in size and seeming shift to career orientation signified by the growth of business programs relate directly to the Saint Thomas faculty development program. In its proposal to the Foundation, Saint Thomas faculty expressed the need to increase communication and to reestablish a sense of common purpose as fundamental.

The program at Saint Thomas was most clearly focused on group activities. The largest sum in the grant went to support summer seminars. Held each year of the grant, these varied in focus and were from two to four weeks in length. Faculty members were subsidized to an amount of about $2,000 for participation, fifteen or twenty taking part in each. In addition, at Saint Thomas, three year-long seminars were funded, each involving three faculty members and fifteen students meeting once a week. A series of in-service teaching seminars aimed at improving specific competences was also funded, but only to a small amount ($6,000) to pay leaders and to pay for supplies and videotaping sessions.

Macalester College

Macalester, a Presbyterian college, was founded in 1874, a decade before Saint Thomas. It retains its Presbyterian affiliation today but sees itself more generally as a privately supported, four-year, coeducational, liberal arts college. Its enrollment is about 1,700, with the largest and most diverse international student population of any private college in the Midwest. The Macalester full-time faculty numbers 117, with a student-faculty ratio of 12.5 to 1. Close to 30 percent of current full-time faculty were appointed after 1978.

The faculty development plan at Macalester acknowledges the more common experience of small, private, liberal arts colleges today: stable enrollments, reduced promotion opportunities, reduced mobility, and some budget reductions. Thus, a perceived need to provide "intellectual stimulation of new ideas and fresh approaches" lies behind features of the plan. As an expression of faculty needs, Macalester's plan reflects individual interviews with the entire faculty. It may embody, more than most plans, some of those features that serve a faculty's perceived needs: blocks of time and other support for research, writing, and course development, support for sabbatical leave extensions, and support for travel to professional meetings or to use research facilities elsewhere. In structure, the plan initially funds faculty grants in several categories: $1,000 maximum research grants, some designated for specific purposes; $2,000 maximum research grants, two restricted to support the overseas apprenticeship program; and $500 maximum grants for such purposes as participating in teaching/learning seminars and coordinating a sunrise faculty seminar. A fourth category of grants provided a maximum stipend of $750 to twenty junior or senior students as research fellows. A number of changes in amounts and allotments of funds were made in the renewal proposal.

　　Two unusual features are found in this plan. The first is that faculty members must prepare, in consultation with the department chair, narrative accounts of their own professional development plans to be eligible for a grant. The second is that some of the money under these grants will be "banked" as credit for additional professional development activities that are consistent with an individual's professional development plan. It is also noteworthy that the Bush grant was designed to mesh with and fill gaps in past and present programs supported by Mellon, Comprehensive Assistance to Undergraduate Science Education (CAUSE), and National Endowment for the Humanities grants.

　　In all three of these colleges, the programs are being supervised by a faculty development committee, with one member of the faculty in each place working part-time as the faculty development director. All three publish newsletters to acquaint the faculty with faculty development efforts and to provide a

wide range of information felt useful to the faculty. All three
are capably and sensitively supported by the administration,
without the administration infringing upon the decisive role of
the faculty. All three programs appear to be working, but with
different degrees of success in their specific parts. Augsburg
and Saint Thomas completed a full three-year cycle in 1984;
Macalester will complete its first cycle in 1985. All three have
received renewal grants. All express a commitment that will extend these activities beyond the period of Bush Foundation
funding.

Together, these colleges define the situation of similarly
located, private, liberal arts colleges with and without religious
affiliation. The size and number of such colleges in the Twin
Cities area make possible the Associated Colleges of the Twin
Cities (ACTC), comprising these three colleges, Hamline University, and the College of Saint Catherine. Students may take
classes on any of the campuses, and some faculty members will
teach a course on another campus. The presence of ACTC may
be a small point of difference between such colleges as these
and the small private college in a more isolated location. In
these three colleges, though faculty members knew generally
what was going on elsewhere, faculty seemed to be little affected directly by being part of this consortium. When the first
site visits were made to these colleges, faculty development
seemed to be very much an individual institutional affair, just
as, to a lesser degree, individual campus programs tended to support the individual faculty member's sense of desirable development. Beginning in the fall of 1983, the faculty development
directors or coordinators of the five colleges in the consortium
began to meet on a regular basis. In August 1984, this group
plus additional faculty members from each college held a successful retreat on "What Constitutes Good Teaching at a Liberal
Arts College?"

Individual Grants for Professional Development

Direct grants to faculty for individual research, course development, or study were a large part of the programs at both
Augsburg and Macalester. At Augsburg, grants were but one

part of the cafeteria offerings, though they accounted for the largest expenditure. The grants given seemed to energize the faculty and connect effectively with other parts of the program. One apparent reason is that these opportunities came at a low point in the college's fortunes. But beyond that, grants in this program seemed well accepted as part of a larger and, at some points, exciting effort. At Macalester, grants were the major feature of the program. Various kinds of grants were administered by a four-person Professional Activities Committee that seemed to site visitors to be unnecessarily small and not fully representative of the diversity and strength of the faculty. Few grants were turned down though three out of five were returned to the applicant for revisions. The proposals, while diverse, were of a conventional kind. Although a number of grants were restricted to certain activities, these did not appear to have yet made significant impacts on target groups or objectives. Direct grants to faculty were not a part of the Bush program at Saint Thomas, probably because support of this kind was already being provided through a sabbatical leave program begun in 1978, a mini-grant ($1,000 maximum) program for professional development, and a Bush Foundation-supported travel fund.

Grants are popular within faculty development programs probably because faculty in virtually all institutions perceive such opportunities to be less available than they would like them to be. Though sabbatical leave plans are in effect at all three of these colleges, the full-year leaves are underutilized. Research or course development grants of other kinds are small and most often present as a result of outside funding. Both Macalester and Saint Thomas have received previous support for faculty development and related purposes from other outside agencies. Travel funds are usually less generously available at these colleges than faculty would like, but that condition may prevail everywhere. Because of low salaries, summers—which theoretically provide the period for study, course preparation, travel, and the like—are used by some faculty to do outside work. Augsburg's salaries are considerably lower than at the other two. Saint Thomas's salary scale in 1981 was among the top 25 percent for private colleges in Minnesota, and Macalester's salaries were higher than at most of Minnesota's private colleges. The small amounts for summer research leaves or participation in seminars did appear to many of the faculty interviewed at these colleges to relieve them from the necessity of summer teaching or other wage-earning activities.

Finally, teaching loads are much the same as in other private colleges—three courses per term plus an interim course—and students and college activities do make great demands on an individual's time. All of these argue for the legitimacy of requesting direct grants in furtherance of the scholarly and professional necessities that are a part of college teaching.

Institutions probably respond weakly to such needs, more from financial constraints than from philosophical principles. Yet, from an institutional point of view, salaries and fringe benefits may seem to cover the minimum expected of faculty: the shaping and holding of classes and the necessary attendant functions that move students from freshman year to graduation. In none of the colleges was there an atmosphere of publish or perish. Though administrators spoke with pride of faculty members recognized nationally or for making some special contribution nearer at hand, the majority of faculty did not appear to be recruited with such achievements primarily in mind or expected to perform in that way.

If, then, the lack of such opportunities argues for direct grants, what do they accomplish within these typical programs?

1. Grants accomplish a substantial amount of what faculty members conclude—for themselves and others—is favorable to their development as teachers at a relatively small cost. The largest of these grants was $2,000, less than a month's salary for many faculty members, and it probably bought a good deal more than a month's time. Most grants were in the $500 range. The other side is that the accomplishments were often small and often what might have been expected in the ordinary course of a faculty member's carrying out of responsibilities.

2. Grants seem to go first to those already teaching at a high level. Such faculty members are also likely to participate in

various opportunities for faculty development whether stipends are attached or not. Occasionally, all institutions report, a faculty member outside this already motivated group will be greatly affected by a grant.

3. Results in scholarly work are usually within a discipline and often attached to research begun in graduate school. The same might be said of grants for course development, though more innovative projects, even interdisciplinary in nature, may result.

4. Grants receive almost universal praise from faculty. They always achieve results in the general ways of raising self-esteem, accomplishing deferred tasks, linking one scholar with others, and suggesting further activities. At best, even specialized work is perceived as having an impact on the functioning of the professor as a whole. At worst, some self-deception may reside in failing to perceive that some academic work has little or even a negative impact on teaching. The balance in these colleges seems clearly on the side of whole and beneficial development. As one faculty member wrote, "I view my professional development as all of a piece and seldom attempt to differentiate roles or activities into traditional categories of teaching, scholarly activity, and service."

5. Individual grants can have a collective impact. The lecture series at Augsburg is an example. Both students and faculty attended, despite the uneven quality of presentations, and most regarded the series favorably. Similarly, grants within the other programs' activities have made the work of faculty members visible across the campus. Earmarked grants for participation in seminars and workshops have had an obvious collective effect.

6. Without adversely affecting the response of faculty, grants can be targeted, as many of these were, for specific educational purposes. With reasonable monitoring, grants can be shifted to meet specific needs for specific cohorts of faculty.

7. The mechanisms for awarding grants were well accepted by the faculty and gratefully acknowledged. This may speak

both to the variety and intensity of needs, but it may also speak to the effects of tangible recognition of what is entailed in teaching beside meeting large numbers of classes.

As to measuring the effectiveness of the granting activities in each of these colleges, most grants required some kind of reporting or follow-up activity that estimated the impact of the grant. These seem to be well received by participants and to involve other members of the faculty (albeit the majority of these were probably also participants) and, to a lesser degree, students. To some degree, the presence of grant opportunities helped offset the effect of low salaries and lack of other professional opportunities on the morale of the faculty. To a marked degree, grants contributed to a higher degree of professional socializing among the faculty, which may have favorable effects on the climate for teaching.

Grants were not very successful in promoting interdisciplinary scholarship or course development. Augsburg had one interdisciplinary team effort in the first three years. Most grants were self-initiated and, therefore, did not take that direction. Those designed to support creation of interdisciplinary courses were often slow to produce results. The attempts to link student and faculty in research were somewhat more fruitful. Though at first neither faculty nor students appeared forthcoming with ideas for such linkages, the Partnerships in Learning at Saint Thomas grew from six in 1982 to fifteen during 1982–83 and to nineteen in 1983–84. The students who benefited were likely to be those already identified and supported by faculty in their goals. In general, grants at these colleges tended to support conventional ideas and patterns of professional activities.

Group Activities for Faculty Development

Within college faculties, a strong impulse exists to see improving instruction as largely a matter of helping individual faculty members to develop in their own self-selected and institutionally assisted ways. It is assumed that such assistance, usually in the form of individual grants, will have a collective impact.

Activities that bring faculty together or that are aimed at groups of faculty, however, are also prominent in faculty development programs. Group activities include lectures, workshops and seminars, informal discussions, course or instructional development teams, and retreats. Most of the Bush programs embraced both individual and group efforts. Saint Thomas's program most clearly focused on group activities. Augsburg's cafeteria offerings included many such activities, and Macalester's grant program subsidized both preparation of and participation in colloquia as well as sponsored luncheon gatherings to hear reports of individual grants.

Saint Thomas. The largest amount of money in this grant went to support summer seminars. Held each year of the grant, these varied in focus and were from two to four weeks in length. Faculty members were subsidized to an amount of about $1,500 for participation, fifteen or twenty taking part in each. In addition, at Saint Thomas, three year-long seminars were funded, each involving three faculty members and fifteen students meeting once a week. A series of in-service teaching seminars aimed at improving specific competences was also funded, but only to a small amount ($6,000) to pay leaders and to pay for supplies and videotaping sessions.

Interviews and other documentation indicate that the 1982 summer seminar led by David Porter of Carleton College was a great success. People became aware of what others were doing, the examination of introductory courses provided a practical and engaging focus, and the group concluded with a set of recommendations that could have specific outcomes. In addition, all participants interviewed spoke of the individual impact on their own teaching and of the value of informal conversations extending beyond the seminar. Finally, this seminar seemed to contribute more than any one activity to the visibility of the program and to an anticipation of other group activities. The outside evaluator's assessment of summer seminars for 1982 and 1983 concluded that the seminars were "one of the most effective curriculum and faculty development strategies."

The success of these summer seminars points to some important considerations for involving faculty in group activities.

The quality of leadership is vital, as is the choice of relevant and important focus and content. The freeing of faculty by offering a stipend is important, but faculty efforts and spin-off from seminars may go beyond the money invested. The Saint Thomas report emphasized both the value of communication among the faculty during the seminars and the ongoing communication across disciplines that followed. In some instances, new course and curriculum ideas emerged, as with Summer Seeds, a program encouraging the reading of classics by incoming freshmen. Finally, as with experiences of this kind elsewhere, faculty who opted for the seminar were judged to be least in need of stimulation. Nevertheless, many spoke highly of the general value of being confirmed in one's established interests and in the carry-over of interest to others. In time, by confining seminars to new participants, at least some of the less likely to volunteer can be involved.

The student-faculty dialogues at Saint Thomas were clearly not a success as planned, for student attendance fell off almost to zero during the year. Here, insufficient attention seemed to have been given to other demands—many, if not most, academic—that had greater priority for students. Shortening the seminars (a year seems to be a long time to sustain interest), finding ways of increasing their tangible value for students, shifting "ownership" more to students, and increasing the numbers of faculty were some of the suggested accommodations. The teaching seminars increased the activities in which faculty could be involved and seemed to function well as a low-key, self-selecting activity.

At this particular time at Saint Thomas, the individualism characteristic of faculties seems to have yielded to a larger impulse for community. Though Saint Thomas's needs assessment arrived at this central theme for its program, an equally thorough assessment at Macalester did not, and that at Augsburg arrived at a variety of needs. Still at all three colleges, faculty did mention a lack of communication and interaction that group activities within a faculty development program might help to remedy.

Augsburg. At Augsburg, group activities were numerous

and diverse. In terms of budget, however, the nine group activities discussed in this section came to about $45,000, as compared with $60,000 for the three activities directed at individual faculty: internships, research support, and course development. The presence of these activities within a small and hard-pressed faculty may account for the superior visibility and impact of the Bush grant here. While none of the workshops or seminars had the impact of the summer seminar at Saint Thomas, none were funded in that way or structured during several weeks of the summer.

Instead, relatively low-cost seminars and workshops open to all faculty on a voluntary basis characterized the Augsburg group activities. In the progress report, most attention was directed to the seminar in the use of computer word processing tied in to increased individual use and development of a computer science major. Additional activities of this kind are planned. The major teaching workshop on library-based course instruction seemed limited in its application but was well received. The teaching workshop activities related to three convocations on "Improvement of the Intellectual Climate on Campus" and the faculty lecture series got higher marks. Both seem to have reached students directly, the first by way of continuing activities of examining the junior/senior year, and the second by arousing both student and faculty participation and interest. The department and divisional retreats received strong endorsement from participants, as did the proposal-writing workshop and the winter conference on advising, and the career planning and publishing seminar. The department leadership workshop apparently did not succeed.

Finally, a modest amount ($5,400) for instructional conference travel exposed faculty to conferences and workshops off-campus that appeared to be of great value and likely to have direct impact on courses and instruction. Several faculty members were enabled to participate in the Midwest Faculty Seminar run by the University of Chicago and funded by the Lilly Endowment. These seminars, held twice a year, have apparently been open to humanities and social science faculty of all these colleges at small cost to an institution (total of $180 for three days). The impact on this faculty member was great, and the cost to the institution was very small. Another faculty member was equally enthusiastic about a conference on teaching world history sponsored by the Air Force Academy, which Bush funds enabled him to attend. It may be that the emphasis upon diverse group activities at Augsburg increased the possibility of faculty members taking advantage of opportunities of this kind elsewhere.

Macalester. At Macalester the amounts for various seminars were small, and the results were not notable. Yet, as at both Saint Thomas and Augsburg, there seemed to be a real general need for more faculty communication and specific teaching/instructional problems that required group effort. A close reading of the Macalester newsletter *Colloquy* leads to these discursive conjectures about the need for and response to group activities there.

If there is a "live" topic in this faculty, it is probably what the liberal arts are and, more specifically, how satisfactory is the Macalester curriculum and the way it is being carried out. This debate in *Colloquy,* engendered by a classics professor and joined by a small number of faculty, seems to have hit a responsive chord. One of the isues of *Colloquy* noted that "during the last two decades the Macalester faculty has infrequently discussed issues that concern and divide us . . . we do not as a faculty engage in open discussion." Though the newsletter has initiated discussion, it did not appear that the faculty development plan had greatly energized the faculty. Despite the emphasis upon individual grants, responses to the second round of grants were slow in coming from the faculty. Experience with other successful grant activities stress the importance of a grants committee stimulating grants as well as processing applications.

The quality and kind of grants at Macalester raised the general question of whether support for conventional faculty academic pursuits might or might not improve teaching. Nor does the specialized nature of such research as aluminum plate lithography, microcomputers in biology, and lab techniques for gel electrophoresis seem likely to provide broadly stimulating topics for faculty gatherings.

A more direct impact on student learning was attempted in linking a student or students with a faculty member in a research project. The idea was popular at Macalester and appeared in other Bush programs. The response, however, was disappointing, perhaps because of insufficient efforts to make the opportunities known to the students or the students' reluctance to apply. In the renewal proposals, applications will be prepared by both the faculty member and the student. Other reservations about this activity also arise; chief among these is that it is principally applicable to the sciences and that it affects, at best, a small number of students. In general, the Macalester program seemed weakened by activities that in theory appeared to be useful and acceptable to faculty but that were not brought very effectively into practice. This may be an aspect of the general tendency of faculties to function within disciplines, majors, and departments, and thus remain relatively unresponsive to new ideas and larger concerns.

An interview with one of the members of the faculty activities committee helped explain some of the lack of impact felt in the Macalester program. Difficulties in identifying key themes and problems in the initial proposal were traced to the strong personality and fixed ideas of a specific faculty member. In small colleges, planning programs is always subject to such influences and conflicts. At best, consensus may be achieved despite a long and exhausting process; at worst, a plan emerges that shows the marks of a small number of individuals getting their way rather than the benefits of group discussion about both means and ends arriving at a consensus.

Direct Course Development

Though the development of new courses and improvement of existing ones can follow from both individual and group activities of faculty, that is more a possibility than a certainty. Built into each of these college programs are specific activities aimed at course development or revision. The program at Saint Thomas allots a major sum of money to support the creation of five new interdisciplinary courses each year. Augsburg's program also provides honoraria for development of integrated freshman seminars and upper-division interdisciplinary course sequences or seminars as a small budget item (up to $4,000 overall), and a much larger amount ($27,250 overall) for competitive grants ($500 to $1,500) for course development or revision. Macalester provides a small amount of funds for developing three designated kinds of January interim-term classes but includes course development as one of the activities supported by their large grant ($18,000 annually) category.

How are these efforts working thus far?

At Saint Thomas, the interdisciplinary courses were acknowledged as being "slow in getting off the ground." The renewal proposal, however, expresses the conviction that this activity in the third year is well established and meets a continuing need. Interdisciplinary work faces tough going everywhere. At Saint Thomas, the desirability of developing such courses was linked with developing more faculty communication. The success of the summer seminars may have the impact of bringing forth more proposals, though in the first three years, no interdisciplinary course has actually come about in this way. Interdisciplinary courses, according to the director of faculty development at Saint Thomas, involve a lot of red tape and must confront faculty members not used to thinking in interdisciplinary terms. Although fostering interdisciplinary courses is consistent with Saint Thomas's larger objectives, that kind of course development may be the hardest not only to develop but continue.

Within small budget items at Augsburg, various developments in course revision were going on. Those attached to use of the computer were most conspicuous, but department retreats, outside conferences, and teaching workshops also contributed to course revisions. Specific grants for summer research and for course development roughly divide support within this program. Both appear to have gained a good faculty response. A rough count of grants completed and awarded reveals a slight preponderance of individual activities going into course development or revision. Development of interdisciplinary course sequences is being discussed, and one such sequence is in place.

At Macalester, the opportunity to develop interim term courses provoked an immediate response, but since the first year, the program has had no impact on these courses. Grant activities have, however, led to the creation or revision of fifteen regular term courses during the first three years. The tendency, however, was still to use grants to develop various aspects of individual research and subject matter competence that were assumed to have a beneficial impact on teaching and, to a lesser degree, on individual courses.

As yet, no measurement of the effectiveness of these efforts at course development (at all three colleges) has been made except to record the favorable responses from the sampling of faculty participants. Several questions are useful to raise.

The first is whether the piecemeal effort at course development and revision flowing from individual grants has cumulative effects. Could funds be better spent on targeting overall curricular needs and perceiving individual faculty activities as integrated with larger purposes? The second is whether support of faculty in general ways of improving faculty competence has a justifiably large impact on courses and teaching of courses. If answers to these questions are not convincing, then more direct approaches to course development and revision and to actual improvements in teaching might be justified. A higher degree of integration of course development and revision with other aspects of a faculty development program seem to be called for in any case.

At both Saint Thomas and Macalester, there appeared to be concrete problems with the curriculum (and these probably reflect on individual course offerings) that were only partially being addressed or acknowledged. The question again becomes what we can expect from support provided by outside funding and from the institution's use of its own resources. Clearly, some of the activities fostered by these colleges' faculty development programs contribute to strengthening the curriculum. But, at best they may only provide a spur to making larger issues a matter of high institutional and faculty priority. The strengthening of the liberal arts core at Saint Thomas is one example of such an issue, as is the chronic conflict between a faculty's commitment to student learning and to its own enhancement.

Distinctive Features

Faculty development proposals often contain special features to meet a campus's individual needs. At Augsburg, the most costly and distinctive was the support of faculty internships to increase relationships of faculty with industry, government, and other occupations. A number of these were completed with a high degree of satisfaction from the participants. A close follow-up here would be useful to see what actual impact the returning faculty makes on teaching, counseling, and the curriculum. Given the nature of Augsburg's student body, career orientation in general, and the location of this college in an urban area, a program like this, if effective, has useful wider potential.

The filling out of a professional development plan at Macalester was also a distinctive feature. Faculty members were required to fill out such plans to be eligible for Bush grants. Faculty interviewed, all of whom had filled out plans, thought they were useful beyond their connection with the grants. More data from those who didn't fill them out would be useful, for obviously such a requirement might reduce the number of grant applicants. Perhaps, like specific evaluation of faculty performance, such activities should be an administrative responsibility apart from a development program. The question of their being mandatory, already raised by Macalester faculty members, would best be answered there.

Within the Augsburg and Saint Thomas programs, but in small ways, opportunities were provided for specific assistance in developing teaching skills: at Augsburg in the consulting triads, and at Saint Thomas with videotaping and viewing of performance. In our sampling of faculty, these features were visible and being used. At a modest level, such aids to developing skills might be a routine part of a development office's operation, a useful service made available and likely to get some use at small cost and with modest results.

All three colleges attempted some direct linkages with

student learning. At this point, these seemed to be the least effective aspects of the program. Perhaps this is because this program is identified as "faculty" development or because faculty have relatively little experience in working effectively with students outside course structures and departments. The small sampling of students at all three colleges seemed enthusiastic about these efforts and wished they could be more widespread. They also offered suggestions as to ways to achieve a higher degree of student participation. Involving students more directly in the planning and conduct of such programs seems a useful first step. Some rethinking may have to be done about how responsive students are to a one-to-one relationship with a faculty member and at the point of specialized research. The limitations of and inhibitions toward such efforts are as obvious as their attractive aspects. Perhaps an attempt, as at Augsburg and to some degree in the unsuccessful seminars at Saint Thomas, to shape the campus intellectual climate is a necessary preface to embracing student-initiated learning in whatever form it might take.

An innovative feature of Macalester's plan may escape notice, but it has particular interest to faculty development in general. For their full participation, participants in the colloquia receive a sum of $200, which is "banked" and can be used for additional professional development activities. Thus support for participation in activities of one kind is used to encourage further individual development activities. The idea appears to be manageable and accepted by the faculty. It may be an ingenious and tangible way of multiplying the impact of individual grants. Withholding the full amount of grant until a project's completion, as at Augsburg, has a different effect, as does requiring some public presentation of work done under grants, which is common at most places.

Overall Observations

Group activities are probably indispensable to faculty development that would have an actual impact on the intellectual climate and specific impacts on teaching. The experiences at these three colleges leads to a speculation that a higher yield in cost to benefits may come from group activities coupled with individual grants than from individual grants alone.

Group activities succeed or fail in terms of the aptness of the topic, the quality of leadership, the ability to compete with other demands on faculty time, and the relationship to the actualities of time and place. Topical and limited workshops—on the computer, for example, at this time—could hardly help but succeed, at least with some part of the faculty. It would be interesting to know how well a seminar like the highly successful summer one at Saint Thomas would fare if a subsidy to faculty were not provided. When a seminar takes large amounts of time, some subsidy is probably necessary. Yet, if the subject is appealing, the leader (let's say teacher) is both competent and attractive, and some useful outcomes are almost predictable, the amount of subsidy may not have to be large. For on all these campuses, there seemed to be a strong desire to respond to occasions for coming together. For all the "busyness" of the Augsburg program, the varied opportunities it offered both to learn something and see and talk with one's colleagues seemed to have a concentrated impact.

Group activities must walk a line between subject matter-oriented gatherings and pedagogical ones. Too much identification of either is probably ill advised. That is, a workshop on teaching introductory courses need not be—can hardly be made to be—divorced from subject matter. Conversely, a workshop on a text or number of texts important to faculty and students should surely generate discussions important to teaching. Where this fusion is present, embodied in the presence of the leader, and stimulated in the structure of participation and interchange, the seminar or workshop is likely to succeed.

As seminar leaders are important and teachers are important, so directors of these programs are important. All the directors of these projects seem well chosen, effective, and respected by the faculty. All are articulate, personable, and reasonably energetic and enthusiastic. These would appear to be prime qualifications. None of these programs had a full-time director: Macalester, one-fourth to one-third time; Augsburg, two-thirds time; Saint Thomas, part-time. All three worked with a faculty committee, and all probably did more work than might be expected from the amount of released time they were given. Faculty development programs need such direction; the money expended for these purposes was particularly well spent.

Supporting committees and personnel are also important to a director's work. Augsburg seemed to have stimulated a very large degree of involvement of faculty outside the responsible committee. The development of other faculty to comprise a separate planning committee had a measurable impact. Active committees were less evident at the two other schools, and at Macalester, the small size of the committee may be a weakness.

Bush funds helped Saint Thomas establish a physical facility, Augsburg spoke of a faculty development area within the academic vice-president's office complex, and Macalester's program seemed centered in the academic vice-president's office. The presence of a facility, even as modest as the one at Saint Thomas, seems a wise expenditure of college or Foundation funds.

The newsletters all seemed to serve useful general and specific purposes. They seemed to be read, and they stimulated interest that may not have been aroused by other means. They did an effective job of identifying faculty development with or without a physical office or center.

Applications to Other Liberal Arts Colleges

Private liberal arts colleges with enrollments of 1,000 to 5,000 students account for the largest group of institutions within the Bush program. With the addition of publicly supported institutions of a similar size and kind, the group accounts for more than half of the Bush-supported programs. Because of the size of enrollments in the state universities, however, these colleges enroll fewer than half the students in the three states. In both respects, though varying somewhat from state to state, this pattern is to be found throughout the country.

Faculty development of the kind being discussed at these liberal arts colleges can have a large impact on faculty, the program of instruction, and student learning. Whether a program is financed by internal or external funds, efforts on the scale of the Bush Foundation's financial support can reach a majority of the faculty very quickly. In a three-year period of small grants, an entire faculty of the smaller institutions may be directly involved. Though getting faculty to take part in group activities may be more difficult, such activities also have a good chance of making both direct and indirect impacts on institutions of this size.

The traditional interest of liberal arts faculty in the whole aims of undergraduate education rather than primarily with disciplines and majors makes these colleges more receptive to course and curriculum development. Thus, the relating of both grant and group activities to course and curriculum matters affecting the whole college is likely to be productive. However, faculty members in these colleges, it has to be observed, are little more zealous than those at other kinds of universities to create and pursue interdisciplinary work.

In both these respects, administration and faculty leadership, particularly in working with well-selected committees, can make the difference between a program useful to individuals and one that more broadly affects teaching and learning. Faculty and administrative resources are not stretched so thin as at the very small colleges discussed in the previous chapter. Leadership is still personal but perhaps less affected by the closeness of association prevailing within very small faculties.

Almost all the colleges in this group had received outside support for faculty development and related matters. There were evidences on some campuses that these efforts could produce cumulative effects over a number of years. On others, the efforts appeared to be piecemeal, one succeeding another, with impact temporary and diffuse. While the presence of an outside grant often carries a certain prestige and gives useful identity to a program, a succession of such grants may have adverse effects. The most serious may be the dependence upon outside support of activities that deserve a higher institutional priority. These include not only professional development of faculty but course, curriculum, and instructional development. Faculty of institutions favored by outside funding may become somewhat blasé about such support; those not so favored may become more critical of the lack of internal support. Some observers have pointed out that the record of institutions continuing programs begun under outside financial support is not impressive. One of the crucial tests of the success of the Bush program is whether these faculty development programs will continue to be supported by institutional funds.

With respect to student learning, these colleges can be fairly charged with responsibilities and opportunities not being given much attention in their faculty development plans. The most conspicuous is the lack of involvement of students in the planning or the activities of these programs. Both the size and ideals of these colleges suggest the advisability of such involvement. Yet, with the exceptions noted in the program descriptions, few ideas for involving students appear. Like the frequently expressed regret about the lack of interchange among faculty, this lack signifies attitudes and conditions beyond the scope of faculty development. There are challenges here that directly aim at the ideals of liberal arts colleges and the practices that should follow from them.

Conclusions

First, all three of these colleges can justify the expenditure of Bush money on the basis of need. Augsburg is the neediest and would have a more severe problem with faculty morale and probably in turn with student retention and education if the Bush grant were not operating. Financial strains are not as great at the other two colleges, but the kinds of activities the Bush grant provides would probably not be going on if they were solely dependent on institutional funds.

Second, as with most faculty development programs, the institution itself might have addressed some problems being met indirectly (and even directly, as in Saint Thomas's case) on their own. A lack of funds surely can't be solely blamed for not addressing a lack of community, diminished communication among faculty, and distances created by great changes in enrollment and emphasis. This is not to say the grant is not serving a real purpose. The identification of even such a general problem as lack of communication is probably a better basis for shaping a development plan than the survey of faculty such as was conducted at Macalester. At Augsburg, faculty also expressed a need to create a stronger sense of community and indicated both the usefulness of Bush funds and of "mild coercion" to bring it about.

Third, the question of continuing support properly rests on some sorting out of what has worked and what hasn't. In this respect, as all three of these programs benefited from a planning grant, so their renewal proposals benefited from their experience with and evaluation of the first period of the grant. An example is the inclusion of a writing component in both the Saint Thomas and Augsburg renewal plans.

Fourth, prospects for continuing college support for faculty development beyond the expiration of the terminal grant are probably best judged by the explicit efforts being made by the colleges. Saint Thomas has agreed to increase its contributions to the cost of the next three years of faculty development from $103,726 in the first grant period to $350,340 during the second. In the current capital fund drive at Macalester, a target of $1,000,000 has been included to endow faculty development and curriculum improvement activity. Augsburg, despite its more difficult financial position, has included in the current capital fund drive a provision for raising $500,000 for a faculty development endowment. An initial major gift of $50,000 from First Bank of Minneapolis has given impetus to this effort. But, as the Augsburg renewal proposal acknowledged, funding is not the only necessity for a permanent program. "Commitment from the administration and faculty of the college is essential." An important part of these colleges' activities in their second grant period is careful consideration of the best ways of developing and maintaining an internally funded program.

Fifth—and this includes many of the contrasting features a case study such as this identifies in faculty development programs—there are (1) individual grants versus group activities, (2) grants moving toward support of subject-matter competence and those supporting teaching skills, (3) activities affecting instruction at large (curricular reform, department retreats, and so on) and those confined to course-by-course improvement, and (4) wholly voluntary participation as against some degree of subsidy or coercion. In addition, this study calls attention to (1) the quality of directors, faculty committees, and administrators in achieving successful programs, (2) the usefulness of communication among the faculty by a variety of means, (3) the problem of bridging gaps between individual involvement and collective outcomes, and (4) the relationship between faculty activities and actual impact upon students and instruction.

❧ 7 ❧

Programs
at Carleton College
and Saint Olaf College

Saint Olaf College occupies the high ground on the west side of
the Cannon River in Northfield, Minnesota, as does Carleton
College on the east side. The Saint Olaf campus is dominated by
the solid grace of stone buildings, suggesting the cloistered origins of Western universities. Carleton's campus is less unified, its
buildings a mix of architectural styles, its own grounds moving
out into residential and wooded land. Northfield is still a small
agricultural town, its greatest popular distinction being the raid
on the First National Bank of Northfield by the James-Younger
band on September 7, 1876. Bullet holes are still pointed out to
visitors to downtown Northfield, and reenactments of the raid
take place each summer.

It is cold in Northfield in winter, and faculty and students recognize the climate as they recognize the small town as
a fact of life. About two thirds of Saint Olaf's students come
from Minnesota. Carleton's students have wider national origins,
although about two thirds come from north central states. Both
colleges are highly regarded as offering strong academic programs and a supportive collegial atmosphere. That extra measure of being disciplined by both the cold and the small-town
community may incline parents to send their children there.

114

Though the Twin Cities are but forty miles away, neither Saint Olaf nor Carleton students seem to frequent the cities in search of excitement. Maybe in winter, as one Carleton student said, "It's too damn cold," and when spring comes, why leave the gloriously and briefly blooming countryside?

Carleton and Saint Olaf graduates become loyal and supportive alumni, though most leave the immediate area via the route of graduate and professional occupations. A high percentage of graduates of both colleges go on to further study. Fewer than half of Saint Olaf's graduates live in Minnesota or neighboring Wisconsin. Carleton probably has even fewer graduates who remain in the area, and many go out to all parts of the country and even the world. In many ways, these two colleges fulfill the highest aims of the liberal arts college, providing their graduates with that first step toward careers and responsibilities of an educated citizenry. Education, according to a Carleton catalogue, "involves personal and social responsibility as well as academic excellence." Saint Olaf aims, according to its catalogue, "to offer an education that prepares for self-understanding, vocational usefulness, and responsible citizenship."

Though clearly there are differences in Saint Olaf's being a college of the American Lutheran Church and Carleton's long existence as an independent college, there are some similarities even here. Carleton was founded by the Congregational Conference of Minnesota, and though the ties were never very binding, the college remains aware of a Christian heritage. Students, a 1969 catalogue stated, are expected to concern themselves with "the issues raised by religious and philosophical interpretations of man's relation to the universe." Of great importance to both colleges is the emphasis on academic excellence. Carleton is the most selective of Minnesota's private colleges and ranks high in this respect among the nation's colleges. Saint Olaf, among Minnesota's private colleges, is, along with Gustavus Adolphus, next to Carleton in this respect.

These similarities of place and climate, of highly selected students and faculty, and of emphasis upon academic excellence within the traditional liberal arts make it useful to look at the Carleton and Saint Olaf faculty development programs side by side. Much of what is said here can probably be applied to other similarly selective liberal arts colleges, denominational and private, inside and outside the Bush program, and independent of exact location. Though similarities in programs and in the faculty needs and attitudes underlying them are most apparent, some differences are equally instructive.

Carleton College

Carleton's faculty development program, like that of the University of Minnesota, is almost exclusively focused on directly furthering faculty scholarship. The basic program provides about $45,000 annually for large grants of up to a term's salary and $10,000 for small grants ranging from about $1,000 to $2,000. Both the large and small grants at Carleton are basically in support of research, though some applicants mention the grant activity's contribution to teaching. The guidelines state that "all awards . . . must generate visible products: research papers, artistic work and performances, public lectures, policy papers, a faculty seminar, or, at a minimum, a written report." About six large grants and seven smaller grants are made each year. In four years, awards were made to 48 out of 142 faculty. These grants, it should be said, supplement other funds available through sabbatical leaves and other regular college programs. One, the Headley Faculty Travel Endowment, provides some $21,000 annually for faculty to attend conferences and perhaps present a research paper. The administration estimates that such funds help only slightly more than half of the faculty to attend a conference in any one year. Another, the Curricular Research and Development fund, amounts to $12,000 each year, about $7,500 of which is spent on an annual summer Teaching Methods Institute. Though this kind of support is sought out by some faculty, it probably does not carry as much prestige or provide as large amounts as grants for research. The CRUD fund, as it is commonly called, appears to be the only fund giving direct general support to teaching, though restricted grants in the natural science departments are available for equipment, mostly for improvement of teaching.

Two substantial outside grants were expended in the recent past: $250,000 from the Mellon Foundation for a five-year period of faculty development support in 1974 and a like amount in 1977 from the National Science Foundation for three-year support for the social science departments under its Comprehensive Assistance to Undergraduate Science Education (CAUSE) program. The proposal for a Bush grant concluded that "these funds had resulted in marginal improvements . . . in the situations and capabilities of a large number of faculty, but in only a few cases did these small grants induce the kind of development we have described as our goal in this proposal." It seems fair to say that fairly small amounts within the regular college budget or coming out of these recent outside grants specifically went into development of the faculty as teachers.

At Carleton, the faculty seem certain that teaching is of high quality; indeed, teaching is regarded by some faculty to be so demanding as to leave little time to pursue scholarly work. A good many of the Bush program grants, large and small, were used to finish scholarly work that had been put off, presumably because of the press of daily demands. Though there is little question that Carleton values excellent teaching, the initial proposal mentioned "a kind of involution, where highly concerned and energetic teachers, focused squarely on the immediate problems and tasks before them, give their major attention to refinements of their ongoing activities. These faculty seem embarked on a quest for perfection in teaching, advising, and college service that, because of its ultimate unattainability, traps some in an inward-looking mode that can be detrimental to their growth as teachers and scholars in the long run." Expressed by some faculty, the situation is simply that faculty live in such close proximity to students, and students make such heavy personal and professional demands upon them, that they have insufficient time to produce scholarly work. Both administrators and faculty admit there is "a struggle to establish and maintain a professional identity in a college dedicated primarily to teaching." Both seem to have accepted the need to create more producing scholars, and both argue that increased productivity will invigorate teaching, enhance the intellectual climate of the campus, and raise faculty morale.

There are several dozen colleges in the country similar to

Carleton and many, including some institutions within the Bush group, that have some similar characteristics. Macalester, Carleton, and Saint Olaf all belong to the Associated Colleges of the Midwest, which includes Beloit, Ripon, Lawrence, Monmouth, Knox, Lake Forest, Coe, Cornell, Grinnell, and Colorado College. In visiting Carleton and talking to faculty, students, and administrators, an observer is quickly made aware of actualities and attitudes affecting the college's faculty development plan. Feelings are expressed by both faculty and students that they are locked into teaching/learning relationships that extend beyond classrooms and class hours and that make heavy demands. Second, Carleton, like most prestigious liberal arts colleges at some remove from the great research universities and the graduate schools from which most of the faculty come, finds itself to some degree out of the mainstream of research and creative activity. The initial proposal spoke of the existence of "a culture at Carleton that reinforces isolation from those whose primary job it is to advance knowledge rather than teach it and from the world of affairs more broadly." Third, faculty development at Carleton may face, as one visitor said, "the particular difficulties of working with prestigious faculties whose qualities as teachers, scholars, and administrators are not usually questioned."

There are other characteristics that Carleton may share with many highly ranked liberal arts colleges: (1) Prestige colleges elsewhere in the country set the tone and aspirations of the faculty to a high degree. (2) Severe institutional pressures to publish are not present, and neither are the inducements and conditions that foster prolific research and publication; on the other hand, nontenured faculty are under pressure to publish, and many faculty feel their own need to do research and maintain their scholarly identification. (3) A large number of faculty work in small departments that provide no colleagues in many areas of specialization. (4) Faculty and student bodies are more homogeneous than those in large, multipurpose universities. (5) A spirit of amateurism in both student and faculty exists, as against the professionalizing of academic life in the research universities. And (6) in the sciences particularly, but also as regards library collections in other areas, the physical resources for many kinds of current advanced research are not available.

Most of the faculty interviewed expressed some form of deliberate choice in coming to Carleton, as against opting for the major research university. Most seemed glad to escape the pressures, but many felt they were disadvantaged, particularly when they had strong internal motivations to publish. They felt they got out of touch with their disciplinary scholarship more quickly at Carleton than if they were located elsewhere. Some claimed that research grants and opportunities, both external and internal, were not readily available to Carleton faculty. Almost all mentioned the heavy commitment to teaching, though one faculty member expressed strong feelings that faculty should and could be productive, and on their own, despite student pressures. Most of the faculty said they did stay abreast of their fields.

It is probably fair to say that neither heavy pressures for nor substantial direct support of published research exists at Carleton. But such pressures and such support do not alone account for scholarly productivity within any college or university faculty. There is little evidence that being at Carleton negatively influences the awarding of outside research grants. Faculty come from major graduate schools and try to maintain relationships with faculty there. Recipients of large grants within the Bush program appear to have received a respectable number of outside grants. And though the teaching commitment is heavy, in terms of visible comparative measures—numbers of classes and class hours taught, class sizes and levels—it approximates those of faculty at other prestige colleges and research universities. Given these favorable teaching loads as compared with those at many private liberal arts colleges, the faculty may be under no greater pressure from students than are faculty at the less well-known colleges in the region.

The lack of colleagues in one's specialized field is commonly brought forth as a hindrance to productive scholarship. Faculty in small liberal arts colleges may be particularly affected, but finding same-subject colleagues close at hand is probably not the norm anywhere. Consider some of the scholarly work at Carleton supported by the first round of Bush grants. Few colleges or universities would offer stimulating and active colleagues working on Schleiermacher, trade routes in Nepal, Niccolò da Perugia, and seventeenth-century German broadsheets, to pick at random some of the work done with the help of Bush grants. The degree of specialization is such that finding colleagues with a closely related research interest might be difficult even within a large university department. For most of such research, colleagueship comes by correspondence, travel, publication, and exchange, all largely at the initiation of the individual. For Carleton faculty, colleagues in most disciplines are no farther away than the University of Minnesota; within the range of Chicago, major research faculties and facilities exist in some abundance. Given the unusually high quality of Carleton students, a kind of faculty/student colleagueship might develop within departments, with bright students stimulating scholarship, even of a specialized kind. The quality of highly selected students also makes it possible for Carleton faculty to escape some of the demands placed upon faculty in large, multipurpose universities, where some faculty energy has to go into remedial programs and into teaching classes in which students have a wide range of backgrounds and abilities.

The conditions and attitudes just discussed do not quite explain the firmness with which the majority of faculty say they cannot do productive scholarship as a part of their regular work. It may be that, deprived of overt pressure to publish and the presence of internal funds for research, both to be found within multipurpose universities supporting strong graduate programs, few liberal arts college faculties will distinguish themselves by published scholarly work. In all disciplines and even at most universities, the great majority of published research is done by a fairly small number of the faculty. Carleton College may be asking its faculty to move from the gifted amateurism that values a diversity of interests in both faculty and students to a professionalism that places being a recognized expert in a narrow field above all other values. Though there was, here and there among the faculty, some uneasiness about such a direction, most faculty members seem to have accepted it, particularly as the institution was providing tangible means of supporting their research.

In the first four years, about one third of the faculty have received small or large grants. Just over 60 percent of the grants have gone to faculty members in the humanities, with just under 20 percent each going to faculty in science and mathematics and in the social sciences. Far more applications were made from humanists, despite strong efforts to encourage applications from the sciences. The chief reason given for this imbalance was that scientists are more accustomed to and have more opportunities for outside grants for research. It may also be that in the sciences, these Bush-supported grants are seen as providing broader (and lesser) support than those from outside agencies. A majority of awards have gone to senior faculty, though about 38 percent have gone to junior faculty. The large grants in particular went principally to faculty in mid-career, the ages thirty-seven to fifty embracing most of them. This is the largest age cohort at Carleton, as well as the cohort that submitted the most proposals. Finally, proposals at Carleton go through a formal and stringent selection process, including for the large grants the use of outside reviewers. An examination of these reviews raises some questions about the use of outside reviewers, but the rigor of the selection process probably has had the effect of enhancing the general prestige of the grants, even as it may have discouraged some potential applicants.

From the administration's point of view, the Bush program seems to have gone along very well. The most convincing testimony to its success is the fact that the program is to be continued with support from Carleton's own endowment income. In general terms, the Carleton faculty development program seems to be aimed at strengthening the well-established faculty in their specialized research, more toward assisting them to become fully and energetically professional than toward any other end. In the first years of the large grants, a majority seem to have gone to faculty who were already reasonably productive, though a number of instances indicate that some grants have resulted in a rejuvenation of a faculty member's interest in scholarly work. A significant number of grants went to assist faculty in continuing work begun as a dissertation; perhaps this accounts for a general impression that much of the scholarly work was of a conventional, specialized kind stretched over a rather long period. It seems reasonable to conclude that because of this program, many of the faculty have achieved recognition within the disciplines in which they work and that such recognition has had a positive impact on faculty and students and may have added to the national visibility of the college. What the impact of this kind of individual faculty development is upon student learning is harder to ascertain. Perhaps a longer period of faculty development will show changes in the intellectual climate and in the performance of individuals and departments from which an improvement in student learning can be inferred.

Saint Olaf College

The conditions at Saint Olaf are sufficiently close to those at Carleton and the faculty development program is sufficiently different to amplify this discussion. A major goal of past faculty development programs at Saint Olaf has been to raise the competence of faculty members within their own academic specialties. In 1972, the Ford Foundation supplemented the college's sabbatical program, which enabled selected faculty to conduct summer studies in the humanities. In 1974, the Lilly Endowment supported expanded summer grants for professional development and also established a teaching/learning center, which has been maintained since with college and foundation funds. In 1977, the Mellon Foundation granted $209,000 over five years for a major expansion of Saint Olaf's faculty development programs.

The faculty development committee at Saint Olaf, an elected body of divisional representatives, has a wider scope than that of setting criteria for and reviewing grant proposals. It is a policy-making body also seeking ideas from the faculty for further faculty development and developing various programs involving both individual faculty and groups. This kind of activity centered in the faculty development committee may be responsible for the three major parts of the Bush program at Saint Olaf.

About one fourth of the annual Bush funds ($59,500) was to be allotted to implementing departmental five-year plans, but this part of the program has not gone forward as planned. Another substantial amount, about a third of the total Bush funds annually, provides for two kinds of grants aimed at course improvements. Up to four younger, untenured faculty each year are awarded Improvement of Teaching grants covering the cost of replacement faculty for one course during the year. Tenured faculty are eligible to apply for Pivotal Course Revisions grants, with the expectation that students, other faculty, and library staff will be involved in these projects. These grants are in the neighborhood of $1,000 per project.

The third part of Saint Olaf's program that also takes up about one third of the Bush grant over the three-year period supports interdisciplinary and group activities. One kind of grant is for groups of three to five faculty to hold summer seminars to develop a new interdisciplinary course or to study an intellectual topic of common interest. Another of up to $2,000 is for groups of faculty to develop seminars for Saint Olaf's Paracollege program, a provision for degree work that does not fit traditional majors. A third kind of grant supports campus-wide workshops on topics of concern to the whole college community.

At both Saint Olaf and Carleton, faculty members spoke of the heavy demands their students placed upon them. At both colleges, faculty members are expected to be productive scholars. The Saint Olaf faculty manual states that "while the college gives primary emphasis to effective undergraduate instruction, it holds that high-quality teaching is inseparable from scholarly and creative effort and it expects that members of its faculty will ground their teaching in research, scholarship, and creative activity." Both colleges probably require similar kinds of commitment to service, the engagement in committee work, and professional services on and off campus not specifically identified with teaching and research. By virtue of its religious affiliations, these responsibilities may be greater at Saint Olaf. It may also be that, as stated in the manual, this explicit concern with "the religious and moral dimensions of life and learning" makes Saint Olaf faculty more willing to propose and accept direct support of activities aimed at improving teaching. The striving for national identity may also be less and thus reduce some of the emphasis in faculty development upon the faculty's gaining the wider visibility that more often comes from published research than from excellent teaching.

Whatever the reasons, Saint Olaf's faculty development program is not so singularly focused as Carleton's. In offering different kinds of opportunities for faculty, it inclines to a kind of faculty development activity probably as popular among a broad range of faculty as the availability of individual grants. At one extreme, this is the cafeteria approach, a program in which various needs are recognized and support is provided for a variety of activities, a program that offers something for everyone and for groups as well as for individuals. The opposite approach is to settle on one or a few specific activities that will make the greatest impact—in the instance of Carleton, a focused effort to upgrade the scholarly capacities and productivity of individual faculty members as the best means to improve the academic program for students. Saint Olaf's program, more than Carleton's, appears to be a community effort and more directly related to specific impacts on curriculum and student learning.

To the site visitors at Saint Olaf, three problems appeared to underlie this period of their ongoing faculty development. The first was the acknowledgment of a condition to be found in colleges large and small these days: an absence of a community of scholars, of teachers and students working together toward common educational goals. In small liberal arts colleges, it is surprising to hear faculty members remarking about not knowing what other faculty members are doing, of not enjoying relationships with colleagues outside one's department or division, or even within such units. The second problem was also an acknowledgment by some faculty that some other faculty and some courses, often what the report calls "pivotal courses," taught by senior professors needed revitalization. The third was how to enable teachers to engage in interdisciplinary teaching or to work in the Paracollege as part of their assignment when such work seemingly does not count as much as does specialized scholarship and teaching within a department.

In the judgment of the site visitors during the third year of the program's activities, the first problem was probably being met most successfully by the presence of the Bush grant. "Workshops and seminars where faculty members met round a common interest appeared to be the most successful aspect of the program." Meeting with colleagues in other departments, sharing common interests, exploring in depth a topic, and developing new courses with a colleague or colleagues were cited as beneficial outcomes of workshops and seminars. Specific results are new courses or aroused group interest in women's studies, professional ethics, and "life-style health" as well as developed competence in workshops on the library, computers, and writing.

As part of the grants program, those aimed at the second problem—revitalizing pivotal courses—met with a satisfactory faculty response, despite the sensitivities likely to be aroused when any specific faculty or courses are targeted for improvement. The enthusiasm of an older Saint Olaf faculty member for his experience in examining the scholarship on ethnic literature is an example of this favorable kind of response.

Grants to new teachers for improving their teaching, however, encountered a problem similar to that identified with teaching in the Paracollege. The younger faculty receiving these grants voiced a perception that their not carrying a full teaching load in their department might have an adverse effect on their achieving tenure. In addition, smaller departments have difficulties in granting released time to any of their faculty, since the teaching load must be absorbed by the remaining faculty members. The problem here is not one that grants are likely to solve.

The Paracollege, established in the 1960s, has long had to compete, to some degree, with departmental priorities. Its presence has faced some faculty members with choosing between a Paracollege commitment and department specialization, with a general feeling that the latter was more important to gaining tenure. The Paracollege at Saint Olaf provides programs for de-

gree work that does not fit traditional majors and still appears
to have both administration and faculty support. Though it experienced a decline in numbers of students during the mid-
1970s, it has been growing in more recent years. Faculty members for the Paracollege are drawn from departmental faculties,
the degree of involvement varying from faculty member to faculty member. The sampling of faculty members working in the
Paracollege showed both strength and diversity; a number of
tenured faculty members testified that their work in the Paracollege was a matter of choice and a source of both satisfaction
and professional growth. Nevertheless, the anxieties expressed
by some faculty of the Paracollege and by new faculty over
grants specifically designed to be supportive of their development reflect the chronic concern over what institutions pro-
fessedly value, as against what they actually or effectively
support.

      If there is a lesson here, it is probably that if grants to
individual faculty are to have maximum impact, they must
work in harmony with both the expressed and actual values of
the institution. An outside evaluator at the end of the second
year observed of the Saint Olaf grants that "the benefit to the
individual may not be found in traditional rewards associated
with scholarship and publication but nevertheless recipients
have a strong dedication to serving the college community."
The common problem of what an institution says it values and
what it recognizes within the promotion and tenure system
exists to some degree at Saint Olaf. And while faculty members themselves are involved in the functioning of the reward
system, administrators are seen as playing a larger part. In the
uneasiness about receiving or applying for grants to develop
teaching competence in young faculty and to maintain a distinctive Paracollege, we may be perceiving a weakness in an administration's actual or perceived support of the worth of these
activities. Grants to individual faculty seem both to loom
larger and to arouse more excitement at Carleton than at Saint
Olaf. At Carleton, grants favor scholarly pursuits more than
pedagogy, a reflection both of a scholarly oriented faculty's
conventional values and an administration's endorsement of

them. At Saint Olaf, grants aimed more directly at aspects of instruction do not as uniformly reflect faculty and institutional perspectives.

The outcome of department planning grants, a third feature of the Saint Olaf program, adds to our speculations about differences in faculty and institutional perspectives. The intended purpose of these grants was to help implement department five-year plans, an activity initiated under a previous Mellon Foundation grant. A newly created academic council was to work with departments to integrate their independent planning with the objectives of the college. In the first year of the Bush program, five departments out of twenty-six received such grants, for such purposes as revising the curriculum of the English department and supporting lectures given by national scholars sponsored by the mathematics department. These and other departmental activities did not appear to Saint Olaf's outside evaluator to serve the broader aims of departmental planning. Progress has been made in clarifying college goals, but integrating departmental planning with those goals is a slow process. Money for initiating this process of integration has therefore gone unspent.

It seems fair to say that at Saint Olaf the involvement of departments (and thus the faculty) in long-range planning and institutional priorities was more difficult than anticipated. Still, it was possible through a year of effort in 1982–83 to develop a seventeen-point position statement that seemed to identify, by broad faculty consensus, important institutional priorities, among which were strong sabbatical leave and faculty development programs. The first of these is reflected in the college's request at the end of the second year of the Bush program to add a new category of sabbatical grants from funds not expended in departmental activities.

Overall Observations

These broad questions of institutional priorities and who sets them are important ones for faculty development. What level of faculty development should be expected as a part of

regular institutional operations? Who sets the priority that gives
faculty development a place in the internal university budget, as
contrasted with funding from outside sources? Who chooses
what kind of faculty development, and who administers it? Who
sees to its healthy functioning? What expectations as to faculty
performance might properly be lodged with faculty development and what to institutional leadership and functioning?

The first of these questions is given a partial answer by
the responsiveness of almost all eligible institutions to the opportunities offered through the Bush project. The willingness
to prepare proposals and the acknowledgments of needs in most
applications suggest that the level of faculty development maintained by the institutions had not been as high as desired. This
conclusion is also supported by the fact that many institutions
had had some faculty development efforts in the past supported
by outside grants. Few institutions, of course, did not expend
some internal funds on aspects of faculty development, though
more ambitious efforts were almost always supported by outside funds. (Of two institutions, at least one of the site visitors
entertained the notion that the faculty might be temporarily
surfeited with being developed.) The needs assessments that
polled the faculty and that were a part of many proposals also
clearly indicated that, whatever the level of faculty development, it was not considered by the faculty to be high enough.

As to who sets the priority that might give faculty development a stronger claim on internal funds, the answer might
well be "financial necessities." Salaries must be paid, roofs re-
paired, interest payments met, sources of student financial aid
found—the list is long for all these colleges and universities.
Nevertheless, at none of these institutions (nor at most colleges
and universities) did the faculty have much direct involvement
in setting priorities within the budget. As to outside funding,
though the administration was chiefly the point of contact between the institution and the Bush Foundation, the faculty was
in most instances very early and heavily engaged in shaping the
proposal and in the subsequent administration of the program.
Administrative leadership and support, however, were also important to the success of the various programs. A faculty com-

mittee working in harmony with a responsible administrator seems most likely to insure the healthy functioning of a faculty development program. Formal evaluations of programs, as will be discussed in a later chapter, were one of the weaknesses we observed. This weakness, however, did not so much mean a lack of attention that led to poorly conducted programs as it pointed to the difficulties of finding ways of carrying out formal evaluations that might produce convincing data. The final question relates back to the first. Rephrased as a statement to administrators, it might read that a vital function of an academic administrator is to identify, clarify, and be responsive to faculty expectations. A faculty development program alone cannot affect all those aspects of faculty performance that have consequence for student learning. The operation of the reward system, to single out one important example, has obvious implications for teaching, but the responsibilities for arriving at and maintaining an equitable and effective reward system are larger than, and other than, those of a faculty development program. In the Bush programs, as elsewhere, faculty are reluctant to mix such evaluative and administrative functioning with more specific faculty development activities.

Further consideration of these matters will be given in the chapter on evaluation. The Bush programs in general are those in which faculty are heavily involved in planning, policy making, and administration. All of the individual campus programs have faculty development committees, though they vary in makeup, responsibilities, and effectiveness. All such committees necessarily maintain relationships with administrators of the college or university, usually with the academic vice-president or his or her office. These relationships, too, vary. Just as there is probably no best kind of faculty development, so there is probably no best structure for carrying it out. Nevertheless, just as choosing activities that answer to a faculty's perceived and actual needs is important, so is arriving at a leadership and administrative structure that most serves the desired ends.

The programs at Carleton and Saint Olaf, as measured by carrying out of the proposed activities in the intended ways, are clearly more successful than not. Even by that measure, however, the success is partial, a matter of measurable modest gains in some respects in faculty competence rather than either transformation or exaltation. As compared with other colleges in the Bush program, both of these colleges began at a higher level of faculty development and, therefore, their efforts may not reveal as big a gain.

Among the institutions in the Bush program, both Saint Olaf and Carleton have a tradition of faculty development and much experience with outside funding agencies. It may be that these and similar colleges, because of their experience, resources, and standing in the academic community, are at a point where they might be expected to establish and maintain faculty development as an ordinary part of their academic functioning. Were this to come about in substantial numbers of these colleges, their activities might provide both incentives and guidance for less experienced and less well-endowed liberal arts colleges.

Examining faculty development within the diversity of private liberal arts colleges points to two significant matters: (1) the need for faculty to develop programs that are consistent with traditions, aims, and customary operations of the institution, and (2) the difficulty of determining how faculty research, scholarship, and creative work in fact affect teaching. As to the first, a large measure of faculty planning of, and control over, programs raises the possibility that such programs will reflect faculty self-interest more than the improvement of their teaching, the students' learning, and the educational quality of the institution. Put bluntly, a faculty may opt for support of those individual activities that more than any other confer security, prestige, and advancement. Such support gravitates to released time to pursue scholarly interests and support money for travel, equipment, and supplies associated with them.

A related finding in a Canadian survey (Foster and Nelson, 1984) and in Cross's study (1976) of the University of Nebraska faculty pointed out that faculty members generally reverted to the "old standbys of clear rewards, smaller classes, reduced class load, better facilities and released time as the most effective ways to improve teaching." Since 94 percent of the same faculty members rated themselves as above-average teach-ers, and two thirds placed themselves in the top quarter, their reason for preferring grants for scholarship is obvious, if not convincing. At all colleges and universities within the Bush pro-gram, faculty members perceive that released time and support money for scholarship is less than they would like. Levels vary widely from college to college, but among most of these col-leges and universities over the years, faculty development of any kind does not have a high priority in the face of insistent de-mands to maintain faculty salaries, meet classes, and maintain institutions. In some ways, the institution's struggles to meet these commitments is similar to demands on faculty members that they be excellent teachers, admirable scholars, and effec-tive agents in carrying out the college's various aims. Faculty development comes to the private liberal arts college, then, with the necessity of finding ways of working effectively amidst these demands.

The matter of whether activities that support scholarship improve teaching is complex and difficult to determine. Part of the difficulty of establishing even the presence and absence of relationships is in arriving at definitions of quality in either teaching or scholarship. Student evaluations provide one across-the-board measure of how teaching is perceived by those ex-pected to profit from it. Though an exact definition may not be possible to derive from such data, it is clear that students rank-order teaching (1) as it arouses excitement, stimulates, moti-vates the students, (2) as it manifests a concern for students, (3) as it is grounded in a command of subject matter, and (4) as it can be communicated to the student in various skillful peda-gogical ways. Faculty are not in disagreement, though they tend to place subject matter competence first and concern for stu-dents lower on the scale. Disciplinary scholarship clearly is em-braced by the third of these four and may be related to creating excitement and motivation but is probably not closely related to acquiring and using pedagogical skills, to showing concern for students, or to considering the larger aims of education.

One might conclude, then, that by this measure, scholar-ship may be related to roughly half of a teacher's effectiveness.

If we attempt to define the quality of scholarship, we perceive that students, except as they register on a command of subject matter in evaluations, play little part in it. Faculty themselves pass judgment on scholarship and, for the most part, on a narrow basis. In most specialized journals, judgments are based on what the work contributes to the knowledge within this field. Scholarly books receive the same base of judgments. Very rarely, if ever, is the quality of either a journal article or a book of specialized scholarship judged by its relationship to teaching. To be sure, there may be an unacknowledged relationship— estimable scholarly work will eventually find some place in the subject matter that professors teach. If one examines the actual scholarship of a cross section of professors and attempts to correlate it with teaching (admitting that only a very partial view is possible), the relationship is more indirect than direct, and small in effect rather than large. The conclusion as regards the quality of scholarship is that judgments of its quality are only indirectly related to teaching and little affected by judgments beyond those of peers.

Some few other observations may be made. Highly specialized research in a general-purpose college is not likely to have a very good fit with the actualities of teaching. Such research in a research-oriented university may have a better fit, but the highly successful researcher may be in various ways drawn away from the teaching program. There is no argument that teachers should not have a command of their subject matters, though there is much argument, in conflicts over curricula, for example, about what a subject matter should be. Scholarship, in this loose sense, is a requisite for professing. Arguments are sometimes made that research is important to teaching because it requires one to keep up with developments in one's field, makes one less insular, more open to give-and-take among one's peers, increases a teacher's ability to give students insight into how a scholar in a discipline thinks, and keeps the teacher intellectually alive. All of these have more validity as they apply to a student's work within a major than to the larger part of an undergraduate student's education.

That published research of the kind that specific professors do contributes greatly to teaching effectiveness is a doubtful premise. The burden of proof within faculty development would appear to fall upon those who claim there is a tight relationship. Without some specific means by which connections between actual scholarship and actual teaching are established, a development program supporting scholarship alone may not be expected to produce demonstrable results in enhancing the quality of teaching.

One final word: scholarship can be considered more broadly than it is considered here, but as one does so, one moves away from scholarship that results in a tangible product, a published journal article, or an academically respectable piece of creative work. Supporting scholarship of this kind requires some faith in the internal development of the person and more effort to measure actual impact upon teaching. Yet such development may be fully as important as developing scholarly competence leading to published work. A teacher of a foreign language, for example, surely benefits from a period of living in that country, in which nothing more (or less) is done than carrying on the professor's interests: visiting museums, reading in libraries, talking with people, and so on. Faculty members long out of a major university might well benefit—as scholars and teachers—from becoming students once again. A humanist who desires to master a new language will not be able to contribute scholarly work in that language, but his or her teaching and scholarly competence is likely to be enhanced. The same could be said of almost any discipline in which faculty members wish to move to right or left of their own specialized competence. Time to do these things is the main need, some of which could be expected to be provided for within the teaching load. But time of this kind competes directly with the kind of scholarship that goes into published work and almost always to its disadvantage.

The general question of the relationship between scholarship and teaching includes the specific question of the effects of an emphasis on scholarly productivity on other aspects of a faculty member's development. These competences—and pedagogical skills are primary among them—may be just as vital to students' learning as published scholarship. Supporting faculty development that emphasizes teaching requires some acceptance of the belief that teaching competence can be acquired and that giving time to it is as important as producing scholarly work. Such faculty development recognizes the plurality of interests, talents, and instructional needs that mark the faculty of even a small liberal arts college. Development of faculty members in one aspect of their professional competence is probably not as important or as effective as enlarging the opportunities for development of various competences and increasing the interaction among faculty that can affect single classrooms, specific programs of instruction, and the institution's climate for teaching and learning.

Applications to Other Similar Colleges

Faculty development programs at colleges having some similarities with Carleton and Saint Olaf disclose considerable variety. Some idea of that variety can be gained from a brief analysis of what was offered in programs that were not single-focus but that still fell short of being cafeteria approaches. Three embraced specific incentives to improve individual faculty teaching skills. Two emphasized greater understanding of student learning and better advising. Two supported activities aimed at redesigning courses. Three allotted funds to faculty workshops for purposes directly related to teaching. One concentrated on working through departmental and interdepartmental projects. Two included support for faculty research and writing, and two used substantial portions of the grant to support a faculty development center or director. The cafeteria programs also included many of these activities.

As to the effectiveness of one program as compared with another, or of certain features as compared with others, neither the internal nor external evaluations furnished definitive findings. Some general statements can be made as to what appears to work at the small but well-established private liberal arts college:

1. Though faculty are drawn to a program of grants that supports individual faculty research, they are also receptive to grant support of activities directly related to teaching.
2. There are various ways of identifying faculty development activities, but an active committee with a respected and active chair seems to be a necessity. Some grants have supported the creation of a modest physical facility stocked with useful materials and providing a place for faculty to gather. These centers differ widely in the use faculty make of them and cannot, in themselves, be regarded as either legitimating or promoting faculty development.
3. Group activities of various kinds are useful supplements to individual activities. Many of the programs that emphasize research grants also encourage faculty to make their work known to other faculty in a lecture series. The internal evaluation of one program concluded that "activities designed to affect the faculty as a whole have been of more benefit (have had greater impact on a wider range of students) than the activities undertaken by individual faculty members."
4. Few of the faculty development programs in these traditionally student-oriented colleges involve students in any other ways. At one college, a series of student/faculty seminars faltered, more because of a lack of careful consideration of scheduling and incentives for students than for other reasons. Students may be an insufficiently developed resource in faculty development in these and other colleges and universities.

Finally, during the last decade, the majority of these institutions have had various support for faculty development. To some degree, the nature of previous efforts accounts for the diversity of these programs. Previous efforts may have supported activities not included in the Bush program, or, in a number of instances, Bush support has enabled colleges to build upon or expand existing programs. Colleges of this kind have been able to contribute their own support to the outside funding and may, therefore, be more capable of continuing programs be-

yond the period of Bush funding. The most consequential result, not only of the Bush program but of various outside funding for faculty development during the past decade, may be
that of breaking down faculty resistance to the notion that faculty members can be developed as teachers as well as scholars.
The presence of specific activities that favorably affect the campus beyond the impact on individual faculty members may be
an incentive to administrators to support faculty development
efforts.

Conclusions

For all that liberal arts colleges place primary emphasis
on the development of a liberally educated student all face conflicts that mark American higher education and that affect faculty development programs. But in its simplest forms, the conflicts are between emphasizing scholarship or teaching, the
pursuit of knowledge as against its dissemination and application, the theoretical as against the practical, the narrower aims
of academic disciplines as against the expansive aims of American education. Put in another simple way, it is the choice of
emphasizing the scholarly development of individual faculty as
the best way to enhance the education of undergraduate students as against the effort to develop specific teaching competences in the faculty and in the courses and curricula that they
teach.

In practice, in the majority of faculty development programs within the Bush group, both inclinations are present,
though cafeteria approaches are more common than single-focus
programs. Such facts mirror the accommodations made at every
level of higher education between these linked but also conflicting impulses. In faculty development efforts at colleges aiming
at standards of academic excellence set by eminent research universities, the inclination is likely to be toward direct support of
individual faculty and of disciplinary scholarship.

To some degree, all undergraduate colleges, even those attached to major research universities, necessarily emphasize
teaching. But the presence of graduate work, even in regional

universities, offers opportunities, pressures, distractions, and a reward system that complicates and sometimes compromises the functioning of faculty as undergraduate teachers. Private liberal arts colleges like Saint Olaf and Carleton escape such direct pressures. Nevertheless, their faculty members come from the major research universities, and the standards for retention, promotion, and tenure they set are modeled upon practices there. It is acknowledged that teaching and research are related, if not complementary, activities, the more so if the broader terms "teaching and scholarship" are used. But what faculty development in the selective private liberal arts college may have to face is greater consideration of the specific demands and aims of teaching, the possibilities for and desirability of certain kinds of scholarly work, and the relationship of the two to the larger aims of that particular college's undergraduate education.

8

Programs at Large
Public Universities
in Minnesota
and North Dakota

Who would expect the largest single-campus university in the
United States to be in Minnesota? Surely few visitors from
other countries and even few Americans without intimate
knowledge of higher education would guess that the largest single university campus in America is the University of Minnesota,
in Minneapolis-Saint Paul. While Minnesota's claim to this rank
may occasionally be challenged by Ohio State or other large
universities, it consistently ranks as one of the largest American
universities in size, with a total head count, including evening
students, of 64,179 in 1983–84. Many characteristics of the
University of Minnesota could be generalized to other state universities, particularly the Big Ten universities, but it has a number of unique features in addition to its size. Although Minnesota is not a highly industrialized state, the university is in one
of the largest metropolitan areas of the Big Ten universities
(2,000,000 population); thus, it has characteristics of urban
universities as well as those of land-grant state universities.

The University of North Dakota, on the other hand, is an
institution with about 10,000 students in Grand Forks, North
Dakota, a metropolitan area with a population of about 50,000.

Like the University of Minnesota, the University of North Dakota is the largest university in its state and offers a diversified curriculum at both the undergraduate and graduate-professional levels.

The proposals of the two universities for Bush Foundation faculty development support represent two ends of a continuum ranging from the single-purpose program to the eclectic multiple-activity enterprise. The University of Minnesota requested $900,000 to provide sabbatical leave supplements for mid-career tenured faculty members whose sabbatical plans would make a visible contribution to undergraduate education in the university. The University of North Dakota proposal for $375,000 was one of the most detailed requests received by the Bush Foundation and involved the establishment of an Office of Instructional Development, a national search for a director for the office, and a variety of faculty development activities emanating from the office.

University of Minnesota

In applying for a Bush faculty development grant in 1981, the university set forth its view of its particular characteristics:

1. It is a major research university, priding itself on a reputation for quality in a broad range of fields, which "by most national assessments," according to the university's statement "place it in the top half-dozen public universities in the United States."
2. It has rejected the concept of a purely research faculty. Promotion and tenure require evidences of significant activity in research *and* teaching.
3. The ratio of graduate students (7,000) to undergraduates (45,000) is far less than at other comparable research-oriented universities. The university has approximately 2,000 teaching assistants and about 3,000 faculty holding a rank of assistant professor or higher.
4. The university is the only Ph.D. degree–granting institution

in the state and is both the land-grant institution as well as the state university. As a land-grant university, it has special obligations for Ph.D. programs in an unusually broad number of fields.

5. Its location in an urban area and the size of its undergraduate student body make it primarily a commuter university. Only about 13 percent of undergraduates on the Twin Cities campus live on campus. Administrators attribute the low rate of participation in extracurricular activities to the predominance of commuter students. Thus, the academic program, they believe, provides the chief opportunity for achieving personal identity and intellectual growth.

The sheer size and diversity of the faculty (which includes staff at the Duluth, Crookston, Waseca, and Morris campuses) make it difficult to conceive of a centralized faculty development program that would affect a significant portion of the faculty. A central Educational Development Program (EDP) was begun in 1970 at an initial funding level of $100,000. This program has continued since, with an annual funding level varying from this initial figure to a maximum of $406,646 in 1976–77. Originally, it was hoped that EDP would be financed by a specific and regularly budgeted fraction, 3 percent, of the total costs of instruction, and that it would be funded at department, college, and all-university levels. The 3 percent level has never been achieved, and departmental level funding has not become a reality. Approximately eighty projects a year are funded through EDP for some fifteen different kinds of activities. Development of new courses and course materials constitutes the largest number of activities, amounting to not quite half the total number. About 6 percent of the activities during the period 1973–1980 were identified as for course improvement.

In addition to EDP, the university has offered the faculty other opportunities for educational development and faculty research. Estimated expenditures in 1981–82 for faculty-directed sponsored research were $140 million. The total expenditures for selected curriculum improvement programs, including EDP, small grants to faculty in liberal education, undergraduate honors program, senior projects in major fields, improved advising, and others, were just over $1 million. Most recently (1982), the Northwest Area Foundation has funded a program to encourage faculty to develop their students as more active learners. The two major faculty leave programs—full-year sabbaticals at half salary and competitively awarded single-quarter leaves for research—were funded at $4,758,000 in 1981–82.

In looking at the problem of maintaining faculty vitality in relation to the university's specific characteristics and in light of past and current faculty development support, the university concluded that supplementing sabbatical leaves had the highest priority. "We believe," Vice-President Kenneth Keller wrote, "that an extremely important element in the vitality of our faculty is their ability and motivation to initiate new scholarly activity in their field of specialization." Closely related to this belief was the fact that the university's full-year sabbatical leave program was not fully utilized, chiefly, it was felt, because faculty did not feel they could afford to take such leaves at half salary. Only about 90 of the 500 eligible have actually taken annual leaves in recent years. For these and related reasons, the Bush grant proposal focused on supplementing year-long sabbatical half-time salaries by 30 percent. The program guidelines were targeted to favor applicants who were involved in undergraduate teaching and whose work plans indicated how their leave activities would "make a definite and visible contribution to undergraduate education in the university."

The program, funded at $900,000 for a three-year period, began in July 1982. In the first year (1981–82), twenty-four awards were made, twenty-one of which actually used Bush funds. In the second year, thirty-two awards were made, and in the third year, twenty-one. Over twice as many applications were received as could be funded. The total number of sabbaticals taken annually, however, appears not to have been affected by the Bush grants, remaining in the range of eighty to ninety per year. Thus the impact of the program seems to have been greater in terms of orienting faculty sabbatical plans toward undergraduate education than in stimulating greater use of sabbaticals. As was envisioned in the proposal, the university is phasing into the reduction of Bush funds to begin in July 1984 and to terminate in January 1986. Vice-President Keller believes the program can be fully funded by the university after that time.

The university has maintained a regular and thorough evaluation of the program. It has maintained basic statistical data on participation in sabbatical and single-quarter leave programs, summaries of characteristics of applicants and awardees of the Bush Sabbatical Program, regular evaluative reports on the programs, and an extensive report of interviews conducted with the faculty members who have received Bush sabbatical leaves. Among the reasons for not taking sabbaticals, financial burden was given by 65 percent of the respondents to a faculty-wide survey, and family inconvenience was given by 30 percent. Salient characteristics of those faculty receiving Bush sabbaticals during the first three years were: 57 percent were in the full professor rank, and 34 percent were in the associate professor rank; 81 percent were male; about 45 percent had had previous sabbaticals, and 75 percent had had single-quarter leaves; the number of years since getting a Ph.D. averaged about fifteen, and the number of years since gaining tenure averaged about ten.

Additional characteristics, activities, and accomplishments of faculty were identified through interviews with the first group of faculty receiving Bush sabbaticals. Three fourths of the faculty spent all or a substantial part of their leaves away from Minneapolis–Saint Paul or their home campus. About the same percentage (not the same faculty) said they began their sabbatical work almost immediately. About three fourths had additional financial support beyond the 80 percent provided. Those who did not have additional support reported some difficulties in meeting that year's expenses. Most faculty members spent the leave writing, reading, and thinking/reflecting. Slightly fewer than half spent some time learning new teaching techniques, and about half spent some time in teaching-related activities. On the average, faculty members felt they accomplished what they expected during sabbaticals, though slightly less than half said their goals were only partially completed. All gave strong positive responses to their year's leave, two thirds calling it excellent and a third, very good.

If this program had only been a way of permitting faculty members to take a full-year leave for research, we would have recognized its value, but with restrained enthusiasm. What was different for the Bush sabbatical supplements was that special consideration was given to faculty members whose scholarly work had suffered while they carried administrative responsibilities for large introductory courses, who had been heavily involved in other demanding educational or administrative activities, or who had to change their teaching responsibilities due to retirements or resignations in their departments. For those awardees, the Bush sabbatical not only represented a rebirth as a scholar but recognition of the value of their contributions to the university.

University of North Dakota

In comparison with the University of Minnesota, the University of North Dakota is a small state university. Though it grants advanced degrees and has a faculty of which 62 percent have doctoral degrees, many from eminent graduate schools across the country, it does not emphasize research in the way that the University of Minnesota does; undergraduate instruction is regarded as its first mission. Its enrollment of approximately 10,000 students makes it the largest university in North Dakota but among the smaller state universities.

The faculty development program at North Dakota is highly successful and unique in one particular among Bush programs. It is the only institution whose program has a full-time director and Office of Faculty Development. The choice of director, made after a national search, was a fortunate one but does not in itself account for the program's success. Other elements that we have pointed out in other programs enter in, as well as specific emphases to be found in the institution and its program.

The University of North Dakota was particularly fortunate in conceptualizing central needs that shaped the program.

These needs were identified as a broader concept of faculty development, coordination and enhancement of existing developmental activities, and activities to offset a potential restriction of mobility and opportunities for faculty members in the future. The first two of these have special importance for large universities, while the third was an anticipated need common to most institutions in this period but one that has not yet become a fact. At North Dakota during the first three years, anticipated overall loss in enrollments did not occur, though academic units within the university have been differently affected.

A major problem for faculty development at the University of North Dakota, as at other state universities, is that of supporting activities that might effectively reach an entire faculty operating in many separate departments and colleges. With North Dakota's 478 full-time equivalent faculty, 200 teaching assistants, and twelve academic units including colleges of nursing, medicine, and law, the difficulties of establishing faculty development as a central activity are considerable.

Nevertheless, that central problem was tackled head-on. To nonacademic observers, the North Dakota proposal in this respect may seem both simple and obvious. Through creation of the Office of Instructional Development with a full-time director, the existing Office of Research and Program Development would be brought into an equal and cooperative structure under the already established University Faculty Development Committee with administrative responsibility lodged with the vice-president for academic affairs. Figure 1 shows this structure.

In fact, at most universities, such symmetry does not exist. In the original proposal, there is an apt description of the more common situation: "The history of faculty development at the University of North Dakota has followed the typical pattern for state universities . . . understood largely in terms of leave opportunities, support for scholarship, and faculty publications. A truly successful faculty development program will be responsive to two overlapping but distinct faculty constituencies: those persons who would emphasize professional development as it relates to research, scholarship, and creative activity; and those persons who would emphasize professional development as it related directly to instruction and student learning."

Figure 1. Organizational Structure Supporting Faculty Development.

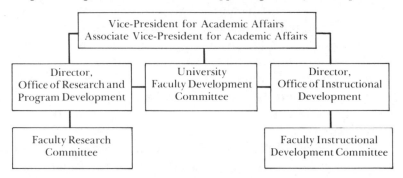

Translated into the actualities at North Dakota prior to the beginning of the Bush program, the Office of Research and Program Development had a full-time director (appointed in 1976) with a budget of $100,000 a year to be distributed to faculty on a competitive basis for individual research projects. In addition, about ten tenured faculty per year were granted developmental leaves, primarily for research. Two other grant programs, one for summer research work and the other for small research projects, totaling about $40,000 annually, also existed. In contrast, the Faculty Instructional Development Committee distributed $10,000 annually to faculty members in support of proposals for improving instruction.

The possibility of moving toward parity between support for faculty research and for instruction and student learning is greater at the University of North Dakota than at most state universities. The emphasis on research-related activities is recent; the amounts of money involved relatively small. In many state universities, offices of research are chiefly engaged in or associated with seeking and managing outside funding for research. The magnitude of such efforts can be gathered from considering just the 1983 research funds from the Department of Defense, which came to $1,795,000 at the University of Minnesota (346th in rank), $23,250,000 at the University of Texas, and $8,745,000 at Utah State, to pick a university of comparable size to North Dakota (Fact-File, *Chronicle,* August 1, 1984).

Nevertheless, administrative leadership, broad faculty support, and with the inception of the Bush program, an office and director of instructional development were all necessary in order to move toward faculty development in which a measure of equality of support and respect was established for instructional development and research. Quite apart from the specific and diverse activities the Bush program encouraged and funded, this move to give legitimacy to instructional development and give it an important, permanent, university-funded place in the organizational structure may be the most important outcome of any Bush program.

Like many of the Bush programs but probably with more bearing upon the general intellectual climate, the University of North Dakota program built upon existing faculty development activities. Grants to individual faculty members were a large part of its activities, the initial proposal doubling the $10,000 annually available to faculty for instructional development. Such grants did not exclude development of subject matter competence through pursuit of scholarly activities but they favored activities likely to have direct outcomes in teaching. In addition, a separate program of "contract" grants was designed to stimulate faculty "to carry out specific university-wide activities for improving teaching and learning." Funds were also used to supplement the university's developmental leave program (ten leaves per year among tenured faculty) in order to encourage leaves aimed at improving undergraduate teaching. A provision for five supplemental grants was made to enable faculty to meet expenses (travel, equipment, and so on) connected with instruction-oriented developmental leaves.

By the end of the second year, thirty-five instructional development grants had been awarded from sixty-two proposals submitted. Under the "faculty development contracts," fifty more projects were funded, involving some 300 faculty. Projected forward and adding in those taking developmental leave supplements, two thirds of the faculty could be directly affected by grants during the total period of Bush funding and virtually all the faculty affected in more than one way by development activities. The only criticism faculty voiced about this part of the program was that grants were often too small to accomplish large objectives. It can also be observed that spread over a six-year period even one small grant per individual may not seem to excessively energize the faculty.

What is impressive about the University of North Dakota program beyond its establishing an office and administering an effective grants program is the range of its other activities. This alone argues for the cost-effectiveness of a full-time director and office. In general ways, the director has served as an advocate, not only of faculty development but of the central importance of teaching and learning. Activities in communicating with the faculty, in increasing faculty interaction, in identifying significant interests and issues are ones that are often absent even on much smaller campuses than the University of North Dakota. The office has also become a place where faculty can go for information and for direct consultation about courses, teaching strategies, instructional problems, and the like. An estimated 200 teachers were served in this way in the first two years. Ways of documenting teaching performance and of recognizing teaching excellence have been a common concern of the director, the senate's Faculty Instructional Development Committee, and the University Faculty Development Committee. Through a separate Bush grant, the director publishes a newsletter, *Plantings,* which serves as the major source of communication among the individual Bush programs. Finally, the office was able to develop additional grant proposals, receiving $212,000 from the Fund for the Improvement of Postsecondary Education to support a project to improve basic skills of University of North Dakota students and students in feeder high schools.

All of this is an impressive return from an investment. Moreover, the various site visits confirmed the energizing and unifying presence of this faculty development program. Despite the active presence of the director and an office, we found no undercurrent of disrespect for the importance of its activities or suspicions about empire building. Instead, the general feeling, as voiced by one faculty member, was that it had "definitely raised the intellectual level of this campus." Three randomly selected examples can be offered as additional evidence: The appearance of *Salmagundi,* a lively, informal xeroxed "sporadical," coming out of the Group for Interdisciplinary Theory and Praxis; a visit by Alvin Poussaint sponsored by the Black Cultural Center; and a Mini-Festival with Ved Mehta on the culture of India, which originated from a modest Bush program grant.

Overall Observations

These two programs at the major state universities in their respective states are significantly different. The University of Minnesota program is a single-focus one originally aimed at meeting a specific and serious problem affecting the faculty: the underutilization of the year-long sabbatical leave that was attributed to its providing insufficient financial support. Foundation staff and consultants raised two questions about the original proposal. Was providing financial support to enhance sabbatical leaves a university rather than a foundation responsibility? Would enhanced sabbatical leaves result in a faculty's professional development likely to benefit student learning? Over the period of considering the grant, the university clarified its assumptions and made evident to the Bush Foundation the severity of its needs. Requirements for receiving supplemental sabbatical leave support were modified to make a tighter connection between the use a faculty member made of a leave and its application to undergraduate learning.

At the University of North Dakota, a quite different approach was taken. A decision was apparently made that a centralized effort to raise the visibility of and expand the opportunities for faculty development could be effective even within the departmentalized structure of a state university of modest size. Grants under the program were specifically aimed at improving teaching, with a parallel set of grants (funded by the university itself) for research and scholarly activities. One category of grant money was allotted to "contracts," which brought groups of faculty together around both curricular and teaching problems.

Site visitors evaluating the two programs felt that the faculty grants at North Dakota were having a greater effect upon the teaching program than seemed to be true at the University of Minnesota, even though the two programs had similar goals and somewhat similar forces operating on the faculty. One difference was that at Minnesota, supplementing sabbatical leaves continued that university's strong emphasis on research. Even though one of the criteria for receiving such support was the possible impact of a leave on undergraduate teaching, the primary goal of most sabbatical recipients remained that of carrying out their own research and scholarly activities. Undoubtedly, their concerns about undergraduate education were reinforced by the Bush program, but there was less direct emphasis upon undergraduate teaching and the variety of ways in which it might be strengthened than in the University of North Dakota program.

Another reason for our perception that the University of North Dakota Bush Faculty Development Program was having a greater impact than that at the University of Minnesota is simply related to the size of the institutions. Efforts such as those carried out at North Dakota would still be a relatively small part of the university scene at a university as large as Minnesota. The University of North Dakota, with little more than a tenth the number of faculty members as the University of Minnesota, provides a much more manageable target group for faculty development activities. Moreover, the Bush program at the University of North Dakota came into a situation in which there were few previous faculty development activities, and it was thus easier for the Bush program to make a noticeable increment in faculty development activities. At the University of Minnesota, the Bush program was simply one of many grants the university has received and with many things going on, the competition for faculty attention and participation was much greater.

But setting aside emphasis and size in these two universities, we think that those faculty development activities that aim directly at affecting teaching competence and performance are more effective than those that do not. Single-focus programs are attractive within large universities where it is difficult to see how any scattering of efforts could possibly affect even a large proportion of the faculty. Such programs are also attractive where a strongly perceived faculty need, such as that for supplementary sabbatical leaves at the University of Minnesota, dominates all others. Many state universities survey department strengths or weaknesses as a way of seeking and using outside faculty development funds. Establishing college- or even university-wide programs, as with current writing-across-the-curriculum efforts, is another way of targeting resources. Obviously targeting of any kind leaves many areas of a large university's total program untouched. Less obvious but just as important is that single-focus programs like that at the University of Minnesota leave a large gap between their impact on faculty and on student learning.

The University of North Dakota's program is one of the most successful of all the Bush Foundation's programs. Its direct focus on affecting teaching and learning, its faculty direction and administrative support, its diversity, its impact on faculty and on the campus, and its likelihood of being continued by the university all recommend it as a model, particularly for institutions similar in kind and size. One reason for its success may be that the climate of the university was especially favorable to faculty development at this time. Perhaps faculty were not as bombarded as at other state universities with conflicting demands and were less self-conscious about establishing academic respectability, less inclined to place doing specialized research above providing first-rate instruction, and more willing to take a broad view of both faculty development and undergraduate education. Perhaps their identity as faculty members of the leading institution in the state rather than of a small state university in North Dakota, of all places, was highly favorable to a wholeness of outlook and a receptivity to serving their students well. The strengths of administrative leadership should also be cited as contributing importantly to the program's success.

Whatever the explanations, the University of North Dakota has developed a strong program and one with a maximum chance of being continued beyond the period of Bush Foundation support. An important implication it has for faculty development elsewhere is the advisability of establishing an office and full-time director of faculty development. In all Bush programs, large and small, the leadership of a part-time or full-time director had much to do with the success of the program. In larger institutions, though, it is theoretically possible for an academic vice-president's office to administer a faculty development program; in practice in these institutions, it is not commonly done. Having a centrally identified office with specific responsibilities for teaching and learning can generate and sustain a variety of activities useful to faculty development. Such extra activities are less likely to be forthcoming from a faculty development committee and part-time chairperson or director, particularly at a large university.

The difficulties of establishing such an office and position probably increase with the size of an institution and the greater orientation toward research. Paradoxically, both conditions probably create a greater need for effective support of undergraduate teaching and learning. Faculty trained in major research universities and pressed both to specialize and produce are likely to be suspicious of an administration's effort to raise the demands made upon faculty for excellence in teaching. To some faculty, funds for such efforts may seem to threaten to diminish funds for research. The kind of person likely to be engaged in instructional development efforts may be viewed with suspicion by some faculty members as not representing a proper academic discipline. To some members of any faculty, teaching is not something that can be much improved on by study or informed practice or by assistance from experts.

Applications to Other State Universities

A brief mention of programs at North Dakota State and the Minnesota State University system will help fill out this examination of programs in large public universities.

North Dakota State. North Dakota State is only slightly smaller than the University of North Dakota; it is a land-grant university and has colleges of agriculture, engineering, architecture, home economics, and pharmacy, associated with land-grant institutions, as well as a college of humanities and social sciences and a college of science and mathematics.

Similar characteristics of size, diversity of colleges, and an emphasis upon research as well as upon undergraduate teaching exist at North Dakota State as at the University of North Dakota. The faculty development program has similarly benefited from strong administrative and faculty support. In renewing the initial grant, a reviewer wrote that "the program thus far appears to have reached or exceeded its objectives as measured by faculty participation, the number and quality of grants, tangible products such as publication and course revisions, and stimulation of faculty activities beyond those directly funded by the Bush program."

Although this program was not administered through an office and full-time director, administration of the program was carefully considered. Much responsibility for the program's success resides in the six coordinators, elected by the faculties of each college, who work closely with the director of special projects who gives overall direction to the program. These coordinators maintain close ties with faculties of their respective colleges and function, to some degree, as directors of faculty development within each college. Thus each may approximate the functioning of part-time directors of faculty development as we have observed them in the smaller private colleges. The Central Program Committee serves the larger university interest and includes the six coordinators, director of special projects, members of the original planning committee, a coordinator from the Office of Student Services, the vice-president of academic affairs, and two student members. Such an organizational structure keeps the program closely in touch with faculty of the separate colleges and yet gives it a fairly large central body to provide policy and direction.

Minnesota State University System. The grant made to the Minnesota State University system was the first grant, and by far the largest one, to be given to a system rather than to an individual institution. The Bush Foundation made the grant with some question as to whether making grants to the individual universities would have been a wiser choice. The success of this grant as measured by its impact on teaching and learning on the individual campuses is evidence that such system-wide

grants can succeed. In addition, aspects of effectively developing and administering a system grant are applicable to many
other public colleges and universities operating under a central
administrative board.

The seven state universities and their programs are described in Chapter Four. In size, they range from almost 11,000
full-time students at Mankato to under 1,000 at Metropolitan
State. Characteristics of the larger individual universities are
somewhat similar to the North Dakota universities just described and those of the smaller institutions to some of the
larger private colleges. Taking in the entire state of Minnesota,
they do not form a closely interacting system, partly because of
geographical distances between them but also because of differences in backgrounds, programs, locale, constituencies, and
historical development.

In what ways did these universities profit from the system-wide nature of the grant? One intangible but important
benefit was the recognition given to faculty beyond the confines of a single campus. The title "Chancellor's Fellowships"
probably gave an extra lift to faculty members on each campus
who received these awards. In most instances, these Fellows
had opportunities to extend the result of their leave activities
to other campuses within the system. In general, and despite
the distances between universities, the system probably also offered an enhanced opportunity for the spread of successful program activities. The Minnesota Writing Project, one of the
strong programs within this grant, originated at Moorhead State,
was established at Winona State, and quickly became a major
faculty development activity within the system. For the small
universities in the system, the linkage with other institutions
was of particular importance. In short, some of the diversity
and collective strengths of faculty development activities were
made available to faculties of these universities as they might
not have been through individual campus grants.

It should be observed, however, that these programs were
as much faculty-owned and managed as any within the Bush
program. A system proposal elsewhere in the region made the
Foundation sensitive to the dangers of a system's administration

trying to impose its ideas of faculty development on institutions within the system. The collective bargaining unit in the Minnesota State University system gave further warning by questioning the initial proposal but giving full support once the faculty's part in it was clearly understood. As the program was developed, each of the campuses had a program coordinator and faculty development committee. The overall direction of the program was placed with the General Advisory Committee that included the seven academic affairs vice-presidents and nine teaching and service faculty. Such an arrangement has worked well, much to the credit of the judicious administration of the program at both the local and system level.

The variety of opportunities within this system grant reflects the needs existing within institutions of considerable size and diversity. It is doubtful that any single-focus program would have had as much impact specifically directed at undergraduate education. Within the universities in this system, the variety of ways of furthering faculty development is unusually large. They include ways of recognizing teaching and scholarship, of getting faculty together to confront various aspects of curriculum and teaching, of bringing visitors to campus and supporting faculty travel and internships elsewhere, of promoting the writing project and other workshops, and of providing direct grants for a variety of purposes. Most of the activities to be found in the entire Bush program are present on these campuses. Similar direct grant programs administered from a state board, as in California and Oregon, have been well received, but the active involvement of faculty committees on each campus in promoting and administering these grants has made an additional impact. In sum, the success of this program strengthens the argument for faculty development that serves a variety of needs.

Conclusions

Faculty development, as seen in these examples, can be successful in large colleges and universities and carried out successfully in a variety of ways. The key considerations may be the same as for smaller colleges: a recognition and responsiveness to individual and institutional needs, an awareness and respect for the nature of the faculty for whom the program is designed, strong and wise leadership within both the administration and faculty, and support of activities that have both direct and indirect relationship to the aims for improving student learning. As faculties in the large public universities are oriented toward specialized research, so must faculty development programs that emphasize teaching find ways to declare the value of teaching, ways it might be improved upon, and means to assist faculty in carrying out both scholarly and instructional responsibilities. In addition, finding specific ways to affect the large numbers of faculty strongly identified with different colleges and departments may be the most difficult problem faculty development in the large universities faces.

Part Three

Effective Faculty
Development Programs:
Conclusions
and Recommendations

Faculty concerns and attitudes are crucial to the ends faculty development tries to achieve. Although we met a dozen or more faculty members in the course of each site visit and several hundred in the course of our many visits, we still wanted to do some broader sampling of faculty characteristics and attitudes. The results of a questionnaire circulated among a random sampling of the entire faculty cohort are discussed in this concluding section. An encouraging fact emerging from the surveys was that faculty members express a high degree of satisfaction with their work. At a time when it is commonly assumed that faculty morale is low, the morale of faculty at these institutions appeared to be remarkably high.

Our evaluation of the Bush Foundation Faculty Development Program also considers the possibilities and difficulties of evaluating similar kinds of programs. The difficulties of producing quantitative data have not kept us from seeking and analyzing a wide variety of information from our site visits and those of the staff and other consultants, from the overall faculty questionnaire, from the evaluations that were a part of each individual program's activities, and from various informational materials generated by the individual programs. We recognize that the greatest difficulty arises from trying to assess what impact faculty development activities have on student learning. Some assessment is possible, both by inference from data about faculty and from the presence of specific activities directly affecting instruction. Among the Bush program activities, developing and revising courses, acquiring new or different teaching skills, gaining information about how students learn, improving advising procedures, observing and being observed by other teachers, acquiring knowledge of a new field, and improving scholarly competence are documentable in kind, number, and quality. That they constitute changes likely to be beneficial to instruction appears to be a sound premise.

By the various measures we use, the Bush program is a successful one. Faculty development in the institutions participating has made a difference. In the opinion of the Bush Foundation staff who worked closely with the program, the Bush grants had a substantial impact in fifteen of the twenty-six institutions and some impact in eight others. Our independent assessment reaches similar conclusions. The Bush programs have been rallying points for renewed interest in teaching during a time of considerable need in virtually all of the participating institutions. In our final chapter we discuss what seems to have worked in which institutions and draw conclusions about the characteristics of the most successful programs. We think this structured but flexible faculty development program offers an attractive and cost-effective way of fulfilling the Foundation's goal—improving undergraduate education.

৯ 9 ৯

Importance of Knowing
the Faculty:
An Analysis
of Current Concerns
and Attitudes

Faculty members believe that the faculty is the core of a college or university. While this may reflect vanity more than considered judgment, there is little doubt that the quality of the faculty is a major determinant of the quality of a college or university. Whatever the truth, the Bush Foundation, in striving to improve higher education, quite properly focused on the faculty. In evaluating the faculty development programs funded by the Bush Foundation, we were primarily concerned with their effects upon the faculty. But impact upon faculty is more readily understandable if we consider faculty development programs in the context of general characteristics of these faculty members in the 1980s.

    Data furnished by individual colleges and universities in support of their proposals give sufficient information about the faculty to indicate some common characteristics as well as differences. Most similarities are to be found among faculty in colleges and universities of roughly the same size, and greatest differences occur in comparing faculty of institutions at the extremes of the size range. These differences are attributable not to size alone, but also, in our sample, to the fact that the large state universities for whom research is an inescapable concern are at one extreme and the small liberal arts colleges at the other.

Some Basic Characteristics of Faculty

Generalizations about the entire group need be made with caution, however. For example, most of the institutions speak of the increasing average age of the faculty, but two institutions had relatively young faculty. A median age in the mid-forties seems characteristic of most of the colleges and universities, with substantially more faculty in the ranks of professor and associate professor than in those of assistant professor and instructor by a margin of two to one. The average length of service in a number of the small private colleges was about ten years. These colleges estimated a low rate of turnover, probably around 6 percent annually. With few exceptions, male faculty members greatly outnumber female faculty. Where they did not, it was because of the presence of a nursing program with a very high percentage of women faculty. In general, the better the reputation of the college or university, the more its program is occupied with graduate work. The percentage of women faculty is also lower at universities with extensive graduate programs. At Mount Marty College, where the nursing program is the major program, roughly two thirds of the faculty are women. In general, however, among the two groups of small liberal arts colleges, the percentage of women on the faculty varies from a little over 20 percent in some to about 35 percent in others. The larger public universities incline to the 20 percent figure.

The percentage of faculty holding Ph.D. or equivalent degrees also varies roughly in relation to the size of the institution. In the smaller schools, 25 to 30 percent may hold such degrees; among the selective private colleges and the large public universities, the figure approaches 75 percent. A related difference can be seen in the graduate schools from which the faculty earned degrees. In Minnesota, Stecklein, Willie, and Lorenz (1983) found that 20 percent of the faculty holding doctorates had earned them at the University of Minnesota and another 30 percent from midwestern universities. The University of Minnesota faculty itself accounted substantially for the midwestern Ph.D.s. In the very small schools, few faculty have advanced degrees from major public or private universities; most of the degrees come from a fairly restricted list of nearby institutions. In contrast, one of the schools in the larger group of liberal arts colleges points out that 75 percent of its faculty have Ph.D. degrees with degrees from forty-one different graduate schools, including eight from the Big Ten universities, five from Ivy League universities, and others from such reputable universities as Duke, the University of California-Berkeley, and the University of Texas. In general, the percentage of tenured faculty correlates with the percentage of Ph.D.s; that is, the fewer Ph.D.s on a faculty, the fewer of the faculty will be tenured. One institution did not grant tenure; elsewhere percentages of faculty with tenure ranged from about 35 percent to 70 percent.

Salaries vary among these colleges and universities pretty much as they do across the country. Salaries in small denominational colleges are lowest and to some degree correlate with the size of enrollments. South Dakota's economy and support of higher education create salaries in many of those small colleges that are low among this group and low in the nation. Among the low figures in the Bush group were average annual salaries of $24,600 for full professor; $21,000, associate professor; and $18,200, assistant professor. (These figures and the ones that follow are all taken from the American Association of University Professors (AAUP) "Annual Report on the Economic Status of the Profession 1983–84.") These salaries may be compared with the average salaries at general baccalaureate institutions. The annual salary figures for private independent colleges were: $34,140, professor; $26,560, associate professor; and $21,300, assistant professor. For church-related colleges (the great majority of private colleges in the Bush group), the figures were: $27,920, professor; $23,160, associate professor; and $19,400, assistant professor. By way of further contrast,

the highest salaries in this group's private four-year colleges
were $39,600, professor; $30,700, associate professor; and
$24,600, assistant professor, figures roughly comparable to the
highest salaries of institutions within the Minnesota State University system.

In general, salaries are highest in Minnesota colleges, both
public and private, and lowest in South Dakota institutions,
both public and private. Salaries within the University of Minnesota and in private colleges competing with similar nationally
recognized schools are close to figures at comparable schools in
other states. Faculty salaries at the larger Ph.D.-granting public
universities nationally are just behind those at private universities of a similar kind and near the top of the AAUP scale. Average salaries at the University of Minnesota, Minneapolis–Saint
Paul, as given in the 1984 AAUP scale, are $41,100, professor;
$30,200, associate professor; and $25,900, assistant professor.
The comparable averages for all institutions of this kind are
$39,700, professor; $29,470, associate professor; and $24,290,
assistant professor.

Though exact figures were not available as to teaching
loads, it is generally true of these colleges, as of institutions nationally, that number of class hours of instruction expected of
faculty is inversely related to salaries. Three courses per term
with sometimes the addition of an interim-term course during
the year were common among the private colleges. Where lower
teaching loads were in effect, as at Ph.D.-granting universities,
greater research productivity was also expected. The ratio of
students to faculty at most of these institutions was generally
reasonable in this period with fifteen to one appearing frequently as a norm. Lower figures at some small schools may
have been the consequence of declining enrollments.

The generalized picture that accompanied most proposals
was that of an aging, stable faculty with reduced chances for
mobility. At the majority of these institutions it also revealed
low salaries, heavy teaching loads, and limited opportunities for
professional growth. Despite this, as we shall see later, faculty
morale was high. Apparently faculty in these institutions tend
to judge their own situation relative to other institutions of the
same size and kind, relative to the locale of the college and its

economy, and even relative to the limitations and mission of the college. This may well be the saving factor for colleges dependent on faculty who somewhat temper their expectations to the institution to which they are committed.

Faculty Attitudes

Less easy to identify than these facts about the faculty in the Bush program is the psychological state of faculty members today. In the 1978 survey of twenty-three occupations by Caplan and others (1980), professors ranked at or close to the top in terms of job satisfaction, freedom from boredom, freedom from irritation, and enjoying good health. Is academic life as idyllic in 1985?

Since the faculty development programs that we evaluated were designed to affect faculty members, it seemed logical to query faculty members themselves about the impact the programs were having. A by-product of that inquiry was information about some general aspects of faculty morale in the academic year 1983–84, as well as differences among faculty members in their concerns, their satisfactions, and their participation in faculty development activities.

We had two sources of data. One was site visits and progress reports for each of the colleges and universities in Minnesota, North Dakota, and South Dakota that had received grants from the Bush Foundation for faculty development. The second source of data was a questionnaire sent to a random sample of faculty members at each participating institution. Those sampled were given the option of a written response to the questionnaire or a telephone interview with a member of our staff.

We derived the population by taking a 12 percent random sample from the faculty telephone directories, with modifications for the state systems and smallest colleges so that we have at least ten faculty members from the smallest institutions and no more than thirty from the largest. Our sample is thus not a random sample of the entire population of faculty members in these three states, but it does represent a range of institutions and is random within those institutions.

Ninety percent of the faculty members not on leave or

off campus replied after a follow-up letter and telephone follow-ups to those who could be reached by phone. "Could be reached" is a significant phrase, since we developed a jaundiced view of the value of college telephone directories in reaching faculty members. Some phones were not in service, some faculty members were on leave, and the chances of finding faculty in their offices at any given time was less than 50 percent. Nonetheless, our return rate is substantially better than the 50 to 70 percent returns usual in studies of faculty members.

Morale and Motivation. In the *Chronicle of Higher Education,* June 27, 1984 (Jacobson, 1984, p. 15), Irving Spitzberg, general secretary of the American Association of University Professors, reflects upon his experiences during the past four years in visiting more than a hundred campuses throughout the country. Everywhere he went, he said, faculty morale was low. "There's a perception that things are pretty bad and getting worse." He reported finding a pervasive feeling that the quality of the academic enterprise was being eroded, along with the "quality of life" of faculty members. "People get so consumed by the uncertainty of retrenchment," he said in the interview, "that they stop spending a great deal of energy on teaching, research comes to a halt, and all they are able to do is talk about survival. This dramatically erodes the quality of life and the quality of the institution. Society, students—everything gets shortchanged."

In a national survey of faculty members reported in the November 23, 1983 issue of the *Chronicle* (Watkins), 37 percent of those surveyed reported that their department's performance has decreased due to declining faculty morale, and 41 percent have seriously considered leaving their present jobs.

In our sample of institutions, the situation is quite different. Only 23 percent of our respondents have considered leaving their present positions. Only 15 percent have looked for jobs outside academia, and only 7 percent are currently looking. This result appears to be very encouraging, but it could simply mean that faculty members feel stuck with no options to get out of unsatisfying positions. This, however, seems unlikely. In fact, 90 percent of our 372 respondents reported that they were moderately or well satisfied with their roles as faculty members. The high percentage is less surprising when one realizes that national surveys reveal that over 80 percent of Americans are satisfied with their work (Quinn, Staines, and McCullough, 1974). Only five said that they were dissatisfied. While 71 percent of our sample would like to retire by age sixty-five and 95 percent by age seventy, most (70 percent) would like to continue teaching part-time after retirement, another indication that college teaching offers strong intrinsic satisfactions.

But can we trust faculty ratings of job satisfaction? In the face of all the depressing news about the current state of higher education, how valid are ratings indicating a high level of morale among college and university faculty members? One check upon validity is the relationship between ratings of job satisfaction and answers to other questions that one might expect to be related to satisfaction. Such cross-checks offer encouraging support for validity. For example, we would expect those who are least satisfied to be more likely to look for jobs outside academia and perhaps less likely to get them. Half the thirty-five faculty members who are "not at all" or "somewhat" satisfied have looked for jobs outside higher education; only 11 percent of 308 satisfied faculty members have done so.

Faculty Concerns. The high level of morale does not mean that faculty members are blithely ignoring the real problems facing higher education today. They report considerable concern about "having too much to do" (66 percent); conflicts between teaching, scholarship, and service responsibilities (54 percent); and salary (53 percent).

The concern about "having too much to do" is not surprising in that faculty members work the most hours of any of the twenty-three occupations studied by Caplan and others (1980). We found the highest level of concern about work load to be, not surprisingly, among assistant and associate professors.

The high level of concern about salary is also not surprising in this era in which declining real faculty income is regularly documented in the charts of the *Chronicle of Higher Education.* This concern about income marks a significant change from the

earlier surveys of faculty carried out in the more affluent days
of the early 1960s (Gustad, 1960; Eckert and Stecklein, 1961).

In addition to this distress flag, higher educators may well
note that almost a third of our respondents are considerably concerned about lack of administrative support, and 17 percent
of   the   faculty   members   spontaneously   expressed concern
about lack of resources or facilities. Satisfaction with administrative support was significantly lower at the large universities,
and concern about resources was also particularly marked in
the state college and university systems.

As Figure 2 shows, few faculty members are concerned
about "monotony" or "lack of independence." The lack of concern about monotony also checks with the finding of Caplan
and his associates that the job of the college professor is rated
as being among the most complex of the occupations studied
and that professors are among the lowest occupational groups in
boredom.

Sources of Satisfaction. What factors account for the high
level of morale in these institutions? As Figure 3 shows, our respondents rated most highly their *sense of accomplishment.* Of
the 325 "moderately" or "well-satisfied" faculty members, 314
rated "sense of accomplishment" as contributing "considerably" or "a great deal" to their satisfaction. As our evaluation
of the Bush program activities indicates, these faculty members
enjoy learning. They delight in developing new skills and understanding. Their faculty role provides opportunities to develop
competence and to feel a sense of accomplishment. This source
of satisfaction was rated particularly highly by female full professors.

Clark, Corcoran, and Lewis (1984, p. 8) apply Kanter's
categorization of "stuck" and "moving" (Kanter, 1979) to faculty members. They suggest that keeping faculty moving "will
require the development and maintenance of an opportunity
and power structure that opens career paths, that provides developmental activities, that facilitates lateral movement across
fields if vertical movement is impossible, that involves people in
goal setting, planning, and governance, that deliberately builds
sponsorship ('old hand–newcomer') relationships within the in-

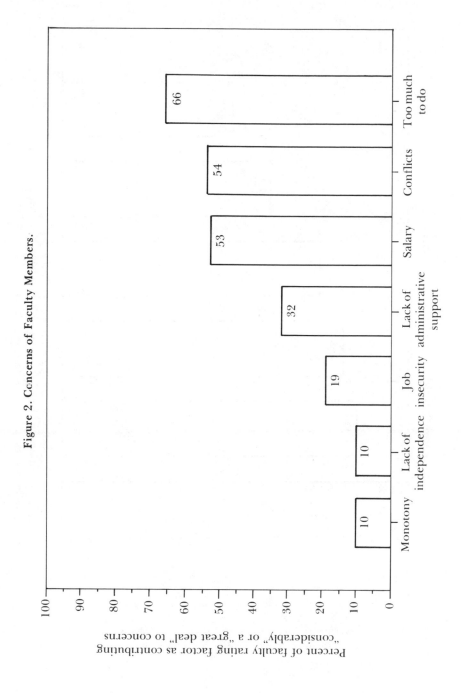

Figure 2. Concerns of Faculty Members.

Figure 3. Satisfactions of Faculty Members.

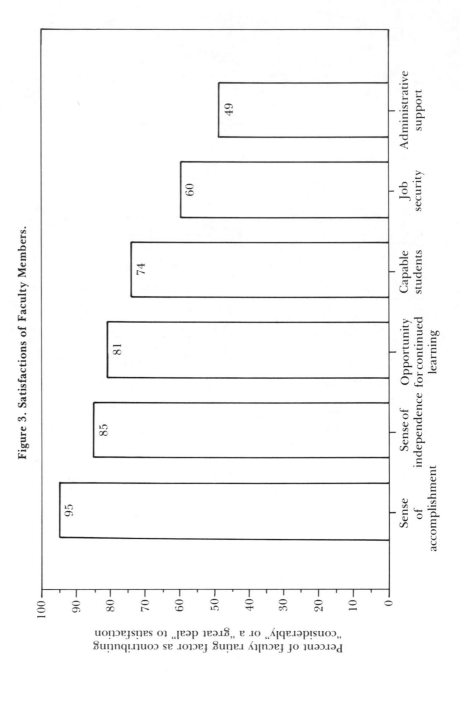

Percent of faculty rating factor as contributing "considerably" or a "great deal" to satisfaction

Sense of accomplishment — 95
Sense of independence — 85
Opportunity for continued learning — 81
Capable students — 74
Job security — 60
Administrative support — 49

stitution, and that recognizes good performance in a variety of ways."

The increasing number of tenured and older faculty emphasizes the need for offsetting the ill effects that can arise from faculty members who feel they are stuck in the same place and professional position. The recent concern with evaluating tenured professors needs to be accompanied by equal concern with positively reinforcing them. The Bush program was designed to involve faculty members in planning and administrating the program. As we saw in the preceding chapters, this intention was carried out and seemed to be a fruitful contributor to faculty morale. In a number of the colleges and universities, new opportunities for leadership and cooperative participation were developed, and new sets of supportive relationships were formed. Faculty grants and faculty reports of grant activities recognized accomplishments. Thus the endeavors funded by the Bush program were well keyed to the motivation of faculty members.

Administrative support is an important aspect of the sense of independence and satisfaction. The colleges and universities characterized by the highest level of faculty satisfaction were those where faculty rated administrative support most highly ($r = .55$); this coincides with our earlier findings that administrative support is a concern for the faculty.

Our study also found (as had the earlier studies of Gustad [1960] and French, Tupper, and Mueller [1965]) that faculty members' *sense of independence* and autonomy contributed strongly to satisfaction, as did *"opportunity for continued learning,"* a variable identified by Eckert and Stecklein (1961) as important to satisfaction in an earlier generation of Minnesota faculty members. Almost half (46 percent) of our respondents were involved in taking, or sitting in on, courses; 73 percent had been attending workshops on teaching; 51 percent had consulted media specialists or other experts on teaching.

Factors in motivation may be intrinsic or extrinsic. Pelz and Andrews (1976) found that scientists characterized by intrinsic motives were more effective than those with predominantly extrinsic motives. In our questionnaire, "job security" is an example of an extrinsic motive, while "sense of accomplishment" and "sense of independence" represent intrinsic motives. When we classify our respondents as predominantly extrinsically, or predominantly intrinsically, motivated on the basis of their concerns and satisfactions, we find that most are intrinsically motivated. There are, moreover, some interesting differences between those whose satisfactions are predominantly intrinsic and those who are more extrinsic. We find that the intrinsically motivated are more likely to participate in Bush program activities, are more likely to plan future participation in Bush program activities, and of those who have already participated, the "intrinsic" faculty rate their participation as having been more productive. In general, our faculty sample's responses accorded with what might be expected from the discussions of extrinsic and intrinsic motivations to be found in "Motivating Professors to Teach Effectively" (Bess, 1982).

While our faculty sample was characterized by high morale, they are not completely free from stress. As we saw earlier, many are concerned about their work load and the conflict between teaching, scholarship, and service. Once again we find the intrinsic versus extrinsic distinction to be useful, for the intrinsics are more likely to see these activities as mutually supportive rather than competitive. The intrinsics also differ from the extrinsics in being less interested in early retirement and more active in seeking outside funds.

As in most studies of American faculties, we found differences between men and women who answered our questionnaire, but these differences were fewer than expected. Women were more concerned about job security, and women full professors rated opportunities to develop competence and to feel a sense of accomplishment as high sources of satisfaction. For the most part, the responses of male and female respondents were strikingly similar. Women faculty members did differ from men, however, in their greater participation in faculty development activities and in a smaller discrepancy between the amount of time they would like to spend teaching and the amount their college expected. The differences between men and women faculty members were greatest for assistant professors. Female assistant professors liked teaching more and participated in Bush program activities more than any other group. Male assistant professors were more eager to spend time on research than were female assistant professors. In fact, the male assistant professors expressed a greater interest in research than more senior faculty members.

Among women there was a marked difference in satisfaction with a faculty role. Women who were full professors were better satisfied than male faculty members; women assistant professors were less satisfied.

As in the case of sex, differences in responses by rank were not as marked as we would have expected. The finding that junior faculty members have more concern about job security is probably more valuable as indicating that respondents answered honestly than as a bit of newsworthy information. Only a little less obvious was the finding that junior faculty members had greater concern about too much to do. The one item on which *associate professors* differed from the other two ranks was in greater concern about salary.

The work load problem is illuminated by responses to our questions about faculty preferences and college expectations with respect to percent of time devoted to teaching, research, and service. Assistant professors would like to spend slightly less than 50 percent of their time on teaching; their colleges expect them to spend between 50 percent and 60 percent, and they actually spend over 60 percent of their time on teaching. (This figure checks well with that obtained in the study of Minnesota faculty by Stecklein, Willie, and Lorenz [1983].) These discrepancies are less for associate and full professors. What suffers is research and service. Assistant professors report that their colleges expect almost 20 percent time on service and they spend about 15 percent (still more than they'd like). They would like to spend 20 percent of their time on research but are able to spend only 12 percent. (This discrepancy between preferred and actual time spent on research is about the same for all ranks.) The differences between ranks are primarily accounted for by the higher institutional expectations for service reported by female assistant professors.

Who Are the Deeply Dissatisfied Faculty Members? Only five of our 372 respondents said that they were "not at all satisfied" with their roles as faculty members. (Because some respondents did not answer all questions, the number of respondents varies from question to question.) Two of the five had been teaching over a decade; two had been teaching only a year. All five were at the instructor or assistant professor level; one was only part-time. Three of the five were looking for different positions. Two of the five were not aware of the Bush program, and a third knew very little about it. A fourth dissatisfied faculty member had been on the committee to write the proposal for the grant but had not participated in any of the activities sponsored by the program. Thus the Bush program did not reach these five individuals.

For one respondent, time for research was the major source of dissatisfaction. For another, the source of dissatisfaction seems to lie more in the location of his institution ("Civilization ceases when one leaves Minneapolis until reaching California").

In rating serious concerns, none of the dissatisfied full-time faculty members listed salary as a concern. Rather, the highly rated concerns were "conflicts between teaching, scholarship, and service" (too much service, not enough research time), "lack of support from the administration," "lack of appreciation," and "the position's monotony, routineness, or lack of challenge."

These individuals were unhappy but had not given up on academia. Although they were actively looking for other jobs, they were looking in academia rather than outside. Two were seeking outside funding for projects; two were working on advanced degrees and another had sat in on courses. Nonetheless, their closest working relationships were with faculty at other colleges rather than those at their own institutions. Thus their alienation was from their own institution rather than from academia. Since these individuals were involved in professional meetings, faculty development activities at such meetings might be more likely to reach them than activities on their own campuses.

Our site observations identified at most of these institutions a high degree of adaptation and commitment to the local campus and community, an observation confirmed by the survey. Causes of such adaptation are not hard to find. Chiefly, the adverse conditions affecting academia are nationwide and, by now, prolonged for a decade or more. There is a greater necessity for faculty to make the most of their present, and possible permanent, situations. These colleges may be fortunate that so many faculty seem to have found local satisfactions countering feelings of being stuck.

The fact that we found so few greatly dissatisfied faculty members sheds some light on the "deadwood" problem. A question commonly raised about faculty development efforts is whether they actually reach faculty members who seem to be most in need of development. Responses to faculty development efforts do seem to come in the main from faculty already performing well. The presence of so few dissatisfied faculty members in these colleges and universities suggests that the problem of ministering to them may not be as significant as is sometimes claimed. One of the presidents in our sample had firmly accepted this conclusion. He expressed the strong belief that positive efforts to affect the great majority of faculty far outweighed his concern for those few who were not reached. A further observation from our site visits is that basic needs in many of these institutions affect faculty at all levels of performance. Reinforcing faculty performing well under adverse circumstances may be one of the most profitable outcomes of faculty development efforts today. Though it does not show clearly in the surveys, site visits also identified more than one instance, and at different kinds of campuses, where faculty members responded to grant opportunities in ways that suggested an unexpected renewal of a faculty member who seemingly had gone stale.

Summary

There is some surprise and cause for further study in the high levels of satisfaction expressed by respondents to our questionnaire as contrasted with general commentary about the low level of faculty morale nationally. One explanation may be that generalizations about faculty morale nationally probably do not match conditions in various regions nor fit from institution to institution. Cutbacks in faculty, certainly a cause of low morale, were a fact for several of the colleges and universities in the Bush group, but other regions, the Northeast for example, have been harder hit, while others, the growing southwest and western states for example, have still been experiencing growth.

The recency of our survey, the 1983–84 academic year, may make a difference with respect to attitudes of even three or four years ago. Retrenchment did not strike colleges and universities nationally all at the same time, but the onset of severe retrenchments goes back for at least a decade. Both faculty throughout the country and the faculty in the Bush program have had time to come to terms with a demoralizing period of change.

With respect to salaries, they are a cause for considerable concern among 53 percent of our faculty, and probably among at least that percentage nationally. The 1983–84 AAUP salary survey conjectures that this may be a period of "bottoming out." For the third straight year real salaries (percentage increase in current dollar terms adjusted for the percentage increase in the Consumer Price Index) rose, though the cumulative increase was a modest 3.2 percent for the three years 1980–81 to 1983–84. For the fourth consecutive year, increases in public institutions nationally lagged behind those in the private independent and church-related institutions. An equally important fact, however, is that among church-related institutions only in those at the top end of the AAUP salary scale (our sample included none of these institutions) did average salaries exceed those of public universities in the same category. Salary data for the Bush group accord with the national pattern in which, below that very top category, salaries at church-related private institutions in each category are even with, or less than, those at publicly supported ones. The gap widens as one moves to exclusively baccalaureate degree–granting institutions. Since the private colleges in our study were with one exception classified as church related, salaries there are roughly in accord with the relatively low salaries for such institutions nationally. That roughly half of our respondents did not single out salaries as a source of considerable concern may be explained both by the general acceptance of a condition that, at least, has not gotten worse in the last year or two and by the traditional commitment to service found in denominational colleges. To a small degree, the results were skewed by the presence of members of religious orders on the faculties.

It is probably only coincidental that the percentage of those expressing considerable concern about salaries was almost the same as for "conflicts between teaching, scholarship, and service responsibilities." Still, if we accept a hypothesis that the presence of denominational colleges in our sample helps explain a relatively high level of acceptance of salaries that are relatively low, we might also conjecture that the conflicts between teaching, scholarship, and service are less at these institutions. The pressure to publish, to put it bluntly, increases in institutions that emphasize graduate work, whether in the actual granting of advanced degrees or in the anticipated futures of their undergraduates.

More vexing, apparently, to our faculties (and probably shared by faculty everywhere), was "having too much to do." One of the site visitors who has been on many campuses for three decades is still struck by the "busyness" that seems to prevail and that is a chronic source of faculty complaints. At the same time, consultants and staff found that some campuses were busier than others. The chief implication this may have for faculty development is that faculty development programs are obviously an additional source of "things to do." The fact that they received such a positive response in the Bush group of colleges may reinforce a judgment that they met high-priority faculty needs that justified the time spent. It might be said that the popularity of grant programs and the difficulties often encountered in group activities arise not only from the direct self-interest served by grants but from the competition among group activities that is a fact of most campus life. One last observation is that serving on grant review committees was accepted by a great majority of those involved despite the admittedly large amount of time it consumed.

Falling salaries, relative to those in other professions, are a fact of life, but the intrinsic satisfactions remain high, despite the stresses colleges and universities are currently experiencing. Faculty development activities that strengthen faculty members' sense of competence and growth are valued. Opportunities to form cooperative working relationships with colleagues and to improve communication are important ingredients in enhancing faculty motivation and morale. Faculty members, despite heavy work loads have an urge to confront larger educational issues going beyond their own disciplines. The heavy involvement of faculty members in planning these programs satisfies important faculty motives for involvement and self-efficacy. Participation in the programs not only strengthens faculty members' identification with their vocation but also can contribute to faculty members' flexibility and creativity as teachers. If there is any one teacher characteristic related to effectiveness, it is enthusiasm. For those concerned about the current state of American higher education, the high level of commitment and morale found among these faculty members may be the most important finding in all of our study.

✿ 10 ✿

Evaluating Faculty
Development Programs:
Do They Make a Difference?

Evaluation of faculty development programs is difficult. While most faculty development programs are intended to help faculty members become more effective teachers and scholars, obtaining convincing evidence of these effects is rare.

Previous Evaluations of Faculty Development Programs

In previous evaluations of faculty development programs, the most common sources of evidence have been site visits by teams of experts and questionnaires or interviews of program coordinators, faculty members, or administrators (Centra, 1976; Nelsen and Siegel, 1980; Gaff and Morstain, 1978).

Useful information was gained from these studies. Centra collected information from program coordinators at 1,040 institutions. Of the six groups of practices identified in the responses, grants and travel funds were rated as most effective.

In the Blackburn, Pellino, Boberg, and O'Connell (1980) report of a mailed questionnaire to faculty members and program administrators on the effectiveness of faculty development programs in twenty-five institutions, leaves or sabbaticals received the highest marks and on-campus workshops the lowest grades. However, some of the goals of workshops and other pro-grams appeared to have been met, with faculty perceiving that they had gained information about teaching resources, that they had increased their awareness of their teaching practices, and that they had acquired knowledge about alternative instruction-al procedures.

In an evaluative study of faculty development grants to twenty leading liberal arts colleges, Siegel (1980) found that the faculty development approach that yielded the highest success rate was professional development, that is, individual research and study projects, attending professional meetings, taking courses outside one's discipline, and so on. In this study, an evaluation team judged programs through site visits and inter-views. Instructional development projects were judged to be least successful. Curricular change was considered to yield a higher success rate than instructional development but lower than professional development.

These three studies arrived at similar conclusions. Faculty members like funds for travel, leaves, and grants. But even though the three studies used different methods, the evidence still rests heavily upon faculty members' own satisfaction, not a completely persuasive measure of effectiveness.

Establishing Criteria for Evaluation

The most obvious and most refractory problem in eval-uating faculty development programs is that of criteria. Faculty development, instructional development, curricular change, and organizational development are intended to improve *education,* but measuring educational outcomes is difficult, time-consum-ing, and expensive. Moreover, educational *goals* involve changes affecting lives of students not only during college, but lifelong. The achievement of educational goals is affected by student ability and motivation, characteristics of classroom groups, and the educational climate, as well as by a multitude of instruc-tional variables. Thus a single faculty development program is likely to produce only a tiny dot on the mosaic of student educational experience. Nonetheless, such dots should be searched for whenever a reasonable possibility exists of finding a relationship between faculty development and impact upon student learning. And some allowance should be made for faculty development initiatives that are difficult, if not impossible, to measure. Programs directed at improving the teaching of a particular skill, such as writing, probably offer the most promise for such assessment, but even in cases where such desirable evidence can be obtained, random assignment to control groups is seldom available. Consequently, we must do the best we can with less than perfect research designs and measures.

In situations where measures of student learning are impractical, must we give up evaluation? Not at all. While there are some programs for which evaluation is likely to yield so little knowledge that the effort cannot be justified, in most situations evidence can be collected that bears a plausible link to intended objectives. While no one measure may be convincing, the convergence of evidence from several sources—each having some probable relationship to the desired outcome—increases one's confidence that a program has indeed succeeded. Thus when faculty judgments, student ratings, administrator evaluations, and expert site visitors' assessments all agree that a program was successful, one has more confidence that the program worked than if only one source were used or the judgments are mixed or negative.

Even such judgments need to be reviewed with a critical eye. Most ratings are favorable. If raters or interviewees are commenting about only one program, a favorable rating probably is less informative than an evaluation in which two or more programs are compared in effectiveness.

Moreover, one must be aware of potential biases that may consciously or unconsciously affect judgments. If one has been responsible for a program, if further funding depends upon progress, if one's self-image or the image of one's institution are threatened, if one simply wants to avoid (or to cause) unpleasantness—responses to interviews or questionnaires may be invalid. Evaluators thus search diligently for data that will dispel their suspicions of biases in subjective judgments.

What can evaluators do? One potentially useful approach

is to analyze the process of faculty development to determine whether each of the steps needed along the way to the final outcome took place. One can analyze what steps were necessary if success were to be achieved. If early gaps in the causal chain appear, the desired outcome is placed in doubt.

For example, let us presume that we are evaluating a faculty development program awarding grants for leaves to facilitate scholarly growth through research. The evaluator needs first to ask whether necessary preliminary goals were met in putting the program into operation. If these have occurred, the evaluator can pursue further evidence related to program impact. The following is an example of step-by-step evaluation of a faculty leave program:

I.   Steps to put program into effect
     A.   How many faculty members applied for leaves?
     B.   Who received leaves? Were they the appropriate target group? What criteria were used in selection?
     C.   Did faculty members take the leaves?
     D.   What did they do on the leaves? Were the activities appropriate for achieving the objectives of the leaves?
II. Outcomes of the program
     A.   Did the leaves have an impact on the faculty members' motivation?
          1.   As revealed by self-reports
          2.   As judged by colleagues
          3.   As judged by administrators
          4.   As revealed by student ratings of enthusiasm
     B.   Did the leaves have an impact on the faculty members' scholarly work?
          1.   As revealed by publications
          2.   As revealed by papers read, talks given, or faculty seminars
     C.   Did the leaves have an impact on the faculty members' teaching?
          1.   As revealed by syllabi, reading lists, examinations or lecture notes
          2.   As revealed by student ratings of learning

D. Did the leaves have an impact on colleagues or the institution?
    1. Changes in curricula
    2. Changes in colleague relationships—informal luncheon groups, team teaching, committee activity
    3. Changes in the institution
    4. Requests for new equipment, library additions, resource materials, links to other institutions
E. Did the leaves have an impact upon student learning as revealed by measures of achievement of course goals?
F. Did the leaves have a persistent effect? Is there evidence that the impact or change will continue over time?

As one proceeds down such a list, the evidence is likely to become more and more difficult to obtain. Nonetheless, carrying out such an analysis gives us some sense of the task of the evaluator and of evidence that may be gathered even in the absence of direct measures of student learning.

Problems of Analysis and Conceptualization

Building upon the work of the pioneering evaluators also requires a more detailed analysis and conceptualization. Research on college teaching has demonstrated that methods effective for some students may be ineffective for others; moreover, what works for one kind of objective may be ineffective for other objectives. It is probable that similar complexities plague the field of faculty development. Programs effective in some institutional settings may be ineffective in others; programs effective for some goals may be ineffective for others. Thus we need to go beyond measures of overall satisfaction with program success to consider what programs are effective for solving what types of problems in what types of institutions with which faculty members. Statistical degrees of freedom are soon exhausted in such interaction analyses. Nevertheless, attention to such variables should enrich our understanding of program effectiveness.

Such analyses should also help us on another weakly developed front—theory. Our conceptualizations of faculty development are not yet well developed. The studies of faculty development cited earlier have categorized faculty development activities, but as yet we know little about how these categories relate to one another, let alone their usefulness in generating hypotheses about what kind of program a particular college should develop in order to solve particular kinds of educational problems with particular kinds of faculty members and particular kinds of students.

In the preceding chapters, we have proposed a number of hypotheses, tentative conclusions based on our site visits and our reading of progress reports, and have made some strong statements about the individual cases described in Chapters Five through Eight. Our basic theoretical model is a two-level one, differentiating change in individual faculty members from changes in institutions. As was developed in more detail in Chapter Nine, we expect individual change to be most successful and enduring when it enhances faculty members' intrinsic satisfactions in teaching, that is, when it contributes to feelings of self-competence, achievement, mastery, autonomy, intellectual curiosity, and engagement.

But change at the individual level is also greatly influenced by a sense of social support. Changes at the institutional level in increased communication, changes in norms about teaching, and sense of participation are thus important not only at the institutional level but also in reinforcing and augmenting individual change. The key to creating intrinsic motivation, Deci and Ryan (1982, p. 34) have written, "seems to be administrative orientations toward autonomy and structures that inform rather than control."

In setting forth on the task of evaluating the Bush Foundation's program, we hoped to contribute toward progress in theory that would be generalizable as well as of practical help in deciding what works.

Evaluating the Bush Program

The Bush Faculty Development Program was authorized in 1979 and the first grants were made during the following year. Most of the grants were made for three years with the possibility of a three-year renewal. Some institutions had completed a three-year cycle at the time of our evaluation but many were in the first or second year of their programs. Thus our judgments of ultimate success had to be made on the basis of partial and preliminary evidence. However, the fact that the program was not complete had the advantage that our site visit and correspondence could have formative effects. We made no effort to be cold, distant evaluators but tried in our visits to be helpful consultants while gathering evidence for our overall evaluation of the initial progress of the total Bush Faculty Development Program.

Our evaluation presents the evidence with respect to five questions:

1. What were the overall results of the Bush program at this mid-course stage?
2. What types of programs have been most effective to date?
3. What kinds of institutions benefited most from the Bush program?
4. Were particular kinds of programs effective in particular kinds of institutions?
5. What factors were associated with institutional effectiveness in implementing faculty development programs?

We had three primary sources of evidence relevant to our evaluation: evaluations by the colleges, site visits, and questionnaires to faculty.

Each college or university carried out an evaluation of its programs. The annual progress reports from the institutions were invariably upbeat, but many provided some documentation for their claims that it had been a good thing for the Bush Foundation to have given them a grant. Although every grant proposal had been required to include a section describing plans for evaluating the effectiveness of the programs proposed, few colleges had much data that we could use. In many cases the program was still in the first or second year of a three-year grant, and a summative evaluation had been planned for the third year. Often the plan for evaluation relied primarily on the judgment of an outside consultant or on the immediate reactions of participants. Sometimes the plans for evaluation were simply not being fully implemented. This is not an unusual phenomenon. Studies by the National Science Foundation and foundation grants reveal that evaluation frequently does not materialize as planned.

Why were the evaluations not more helpful? In some cases there was simply a lack of know-how. In other cases the lack was in motivation. Those directing the program saw little value to them in evaluation; the value of the Bush program seemed self-evident from the compliments of friends and colleagues.

Some evaluation programs, however, were quite systematic. Concordia College of Saint Paul collected data from faculty at the beginning of the Bush program and gathered comparable data two years later. One of the best designed evaluation programs, that at the College of Saint Scholastica, took as the goals of its evaluation "determining if the programs are (a) reaching the target population, (b) providing the resources, services, and benefits envisioned, (c) effective in terms of impact on faculty and students, and (d) cost-efficient in comparison to alternative strategies." The Saint Scholastica evaluators, Chandra M. N. Mehrota and Gloria Singer, collected data before, during, and after the Bush program activities. *Before* planning workshops and seminars, they conducted needs assessment. *During* workshops, they carried out systematic observations to assess the match between what was proposed and what was done. Immediately *after* the workshops, participants evaluated the contents and methodology. The evaluators planned a long-term follow-up of the impact of their program components (small grants, workshops, faculty retraining, and released time). The internal evaluator provided ongoing feedback to the program planners, and an external evaluator provided technical assistance and expert judgment in the summative evaluation. Oral and written reports to the faculty, the faculty development committee, and administrators resulted in changes in the released time and grants programs. (Unfortunately for us, the follow-up summative data are not yet available.)

In addition to the data furnished by the institution, we visited each campus and interviewed administrators, faculty members, and students together with the Bush Foundation staff. We met with the committees responsible for the program. We visited classes. The colleges cooperated effectively in giving us access to anyone, or any data, we wished to see. Although the visits were primarily designed to find out what sorts of activities were working and why, we did not try to be completely neutral observers. Thus we may be a variable to be considered in later evaluations.

Each site visitor rated the success of the program independently. The written reports of the site visits were read by Professor Robert Blackburn of the Center for the Study of Higher Education at the University of Michigan, who had carried out one of the earlier national studies of faculty development. Using the reports, Professor Blackburn rated each project on the basis of the report. His ratings correlated between .4 and .6 with those given by the Bush Foundation staff and authors—a reasonable level of agreement. The site visits thus provided both data for the overall evaluation and a source of consultative help for the institution.

Our third source of evidence was questionnaires submitted to a random sample of faculty members at each college and university (see the Appendix). Site visitors invariably see a selected sample of administrators, faculty members, and students—typically those who as committee members, grant recipients, and participants have firsthand knowledge of the program. Generally speaking, such individuals have a vested interest in the success of the program and renewal of the grant.

While our site visits were marked by openness and candor, the opinions of those seen on the visits could not be said to be representative of the faculties as a whole. Consequently, we polled a random sample of 12 percent of the faculty at each institution, choosing a minimum of ten faculty members at the institutions so small that 12 percent would have yielded less than ten. For the Minnesota State University system, five faculty members were polled from each of the seven campuses; for the University of Minnesota, a sample of thirty was chosen.

Faculty members receiving the questionnaires were given the option of answering the questions in writing or by telephone interview, and almost all responded in writing. Written and telephone interviews with follow-ups resulted in 383 responses out of a total sample of 455. (In evaluating responses to the questionnaire in the Appendix, please note that many questions were answered by fewer than 383 since some questions were to be answered only by those who participated in the program. Also, 14 respondents were not aware of the Bush program and thus could not respond to questions about it.) Of the 72 not responding, 41 were identified as having left the institution, either permanently or for a leave, so that we had responses from over 90 percent of the faculty members in residence. Since typical return rates for studies of this type are less than 60 percent, we were well pleased with the cooperation we received. Interestingly, the response rate in the first month after mailing correlated positively with the success of the program as previously rated by site visitors.

Overall Results of the Bush Program

In considering the overall results of the program, we asked first what steps would have to be taken if the objectives of the Bush program were to be achieved. We then looked at evidence of the effects of the program. We addressed the following questions:

I.   Necessary prerequisites for success
     A.   Did institutions respond with proposals for the Bush Faculty Development Program?
     B.   Were the proposed programs implemented?
     C.   How many faculty members were affected?

II.   What kinds of effects can be documented?
    A.   Institutional effects
        1.   Changes in norms about teaching
        2.   Curricular changes
        3.   Communication within colleges and universities
        4.   Communication between colleges and universities
        5.   Administrative-organizational changes, for example, greater involvement of faculty
        6.   Impact upon overall faculty morale
    B.   Impact upon faculty
        1.   Motivational effects
        2.   Cognitive learning
        3.   Development of additional skills in teaching and changes in teaching

Evidence of Necessary Prerequisites. The response to the Bush Faculty Development Program was exceptional. Forty-one of the forty-five four-year colleges and universities in the three states participated. Moreover, faculty members were heavily involved in developing the plans for the programs proposed. Seventy-nine percent of our respondents said that faculty members had had considerable input and 31 percent had themselves had considerable input. Thus the program met the first test of viability—consumer acceptance. Moreover, the programs proposed were tried, although a few were changed or cut short as circumstances changed.

But having a program isn't likely to be a success if no one comes. Thus evidence of faculty participation is critical. We have two sources of estimates of participation: reports from the colleges themselves and estimates from our faculty questionnaires.

Of our random sample of questionnaire respondents, 59 percent reported that they had participated in one or more of the activities sponsored under Bush program grants; 37 percent of the respondents felt that *all* of the faculty had benefited from the Bush programs at their institutions. We estimate that there are about 8,000 faculty members in the institutions receiving Bush grants. Extrapolating college by college from our sample of respondents and the colleges' own reports, we estimate that about 3,000 faculty members had participated in at least one Bush program activity at the time of our assessment. Many of those who had not yet participated expected to do so in the future; in fact, 84 percent of all faculty respondents had either participated or planned to do so. Moreover, the overwhelming majority (86 percent) of those who participated reported that their participation had been productive.

Thus the answers to our first set of questions are overwhelmingly positive. The response to the program from institutions was excellent; the programs proposed were effected; large numbers of faculty members were involved, and they found their participation to be worthwhile.

Institutional Effects. Evaluations often stop with the findings we have just cited. The numbers of faculty affected and their own judgment of the value of the program for them is impressive. Nonetheless, we believe we can go beyond these data with additional evidence relevant to evaluation of the Bush program.

Our first question was whether or not the different types of programs had the direct effects intended: Did curricular change projects result in changes in curriculum? Did course development projects result in new or revised courses? Did workshops or seminars result in changes in teaching? Did grants for professional development result in scholarly products or in a renewed sense of competence? Our answer to all these questions is yes. New curricular requirements and courses have been approved. Faculty members attending workshops or seminars describe changes they have made in teaching. Writing programs resulted in syllabi showing more emphasis upon writing. Grantees report publications and presentations at professional meetings as well as formal or informal talks to faculty and students on their own campuses. In addition, they glowingly testify to expansion of their intellectual horizons. The individual reports of projects collected by local evaluators provide specific, convincing instances of changes resulting from Bush programs.

Sixty-nine percent of our respondents reported that *norms* about teaching had changed as a result of the Bush Faculty Development Program. The greatest impact was in norms about teaching writing. Fifty-five percent of those reporting changes said that more writing was required, higher standards were set, and writing was taught in more courses beyond the usual freshman English course.

But other changes in norms were also noted by large numbers of faculty members: better teaching and greater variety of methods (26 percent); more student discussion and class participation (25 percent); and changes in faculty expectations of students (21 percent). Also mentioned by respondents at more than one institution were more use of computers and increase and improvement in laboratory teaching.

One may properly be skeptical about responses of satisfaction with programs. But questions about norms seem less vulnerable to skepticism. A norm involves perception of what is accepted practice in one's group. Thus the fact that substantial numbers of faculty members perceive the norms about teaching as having changed is in itself evidence that the norms have changed. While faculty members value independence, they also are concerned about respect from their colleagues and are thus likely to be influenced by changes in norms. Consequently, we view this area of change as particularly significant.

Additional evidence of the impact of the Bush program comes from the fact that at least ten of the colleges carried out *curricular changes* in connection with Bush program activities. Several of the other colleges made grants to individuals or groups of individuals for smaller changes in departmental curricula or courses.

Saint Olaf College, for example, instituted a new freshman seminar, "People in Changing Societies," and new courses and requirements for the majors in English and in classics; Gustavus Adolphus introduced alternative general education curricula and a writing program; Mary College shifted from a subject-based core curriculum to a competency-based core, and, as we have indicated earlier, at least a dozen colleges introduced major changes in their writing programs.

While we have no conclusive evidence that such changes in curricula result in a better education for students, it is reasonable to believe that groups of competent faculty members will develop new courses and curricula that in some ways better represent the present state of knowledge and thinking than did the older course structures.

Moreover, curricular changes inevitably have other effects. Faculty members are motivated by new challenges, and teaching a newly revised course is likely to renew freshness and enthusiasm. Further, thinking through changes in curricula and courses is an educational activity for faculty members. Our respondents reported that they learned from one another about related areas of learning and new developments in theory and research. Finally, work on curricula helped develop communication among faculty, the absence of which was deplored by many faculty members in these colleges and universities.

An anonymous philosophy professor wrote, "In the department projects I was stimulated to think about, discuss, and introduce into my teaching areas of philosophy and ideas that I would not otherwise have studied as fruitfully. The interdisciplinary summer seminars were extremely stimulating and led to much faculty cooperation. I have taught courses or parts of courses with five other colleagues as a result of the Bush programs and have involved at least ten other people in my teaching. Only rarely has ignorance of others' work turned into contempt."

The Bush Foundation grants also affected *communication*. They undoubtedly had an impact upon communication *between* institutions. The annual conference conducted by Dr. Robert Young of the University of North Dakota brought together those responsible for the Bush programs in most of the participating institutions—an event that was mentioned favorably by a number of the participants.

In addition, several grants directly involved interactions with other institutions. Colleges called in consultants from other colleges and universities in the region and some of these ties continue. The Minnesota State University grant not only facilitated communication between the state universities but also is reported to have had a favorable effect on relations between the central administration and the local institutions. In addition, the experience of working together on the Bush program moderated adversarial relations between the administration and the faculty union. This seemed to be true not only on the unionized campuses, for respondents at other colleges mentioned the program's positive impact on communication between faculty and administrators.

Did the grants affect communication patterns *within* institutions? The majority of faculty members responding to our questionnaire (58 percent) answered yes to this question. They particularly cited increases in interdisciplinary communication. In fact, 17 percent of the respondents felt that getting to know other faculty members was one of the primary benefits of their participation in Bush program activities. Blackburn, Pellino, Boberg, and O'Connell (1980) found a similar result in their study. Moreover, the benefits extended beyond communication. Ten of our respondents reported new patterns of collaboration as a result of their participation. Concordia College of Saint Paul carried out a survey of their faculty both just before the Bush program and two years later. The results showed increased trust and mutual respect. Snyder and Morris (1984) found that the quality of communication was strongly related to organizational performance in government organizations. Institutions of higher education seem likely to produce similar patterns.

Documentary evidence of increased communication is to be found in the "newsletters" of various kinds that were begun in the majority of institutions. These ranged from handsomely printed and illustrated publications from the Minnesota State University system to a number of informal publications that used part of their pages to conduct dialogues about educational issues. In addition, a publication, *Plantings*, from the University of North Dakota program circulated notices and news of Bush project activities among all the institutions in the project.

What effect did the grants have upon college *organization* or administration? In most of the grantee institutions, the Bush grant was administered by a faculty committee. In some colleges, a new center or new position was created.

Money brings influence, even in academia, and these faculty committees or faculty development coordinators became important parts of the organizational structure. In most colleges, the grants seem to have increased faculty power, or at least faculty members' perception of influence. In one college, the president turned so much authority over to the faculty committee that he complained about not being able to use Bush funds for needs he considered to be of high priority. Nonetheless, the perception of greater faculty influence may not have been at the expense of administrators. Faculty members reported better communication with administrators resulting from the grant. The Bush grants redounded to administrators' credit both in terms of their ability to get the grant and their wisdom in turning grant administration over to the faculty. As we saw earlier, 79 percent of our respondents reported that faculty members had "considerable" or "a great deal" of input into the Bush programs at their colleges. In some situations, we may have the paradoxical result of both administration and faculty achieving greater influence, the consequence of reduced conflict and greater credibility.

In addition to the direct effects of involvement in developing the Bush program, other organizational changes evolved as the programs developed. Curriculum revision projects sometimes resulted in new structures for monitoring the curriculum and in reorganizations of departmental or divisional structure. New faculty leaders emerged. Changes in one area of a college have ripple effects in other areas.

A dominant theme in our site visits was the positive effect of the Bush program upon faculty *morale*. For some institutions, receiving a grant was important as a sign of viability and outside recognition of their value. For others, it gave promise of activities that faculty members had identified as important for their own development—a positive element in a situation that otherwise was often marked by negative news about budgets and enrollment.

Despite the national news of gloom, morale in these institutions is generally good. Ninety percent of our respondents reported that they were well satisfied with their roles as faculty members—a figure that is at least not contradictory to the hypothesis that there were favorable effects of the Bush program.

Many faculty members and administrators reported that the Bush grant had been a significant source of hope in the midst of otherwise depressing times.

Institutional commitment to faculty development appears to have been altered by the Bush grants. Probably the most convincing evidence of the Bush program's value is the decision of administrators and boards of trustees to put their own funds into continuation of the faculty development programs. As we have seen, almost all of these institutions have been facing severe budgetary problems. After the first eighteen months of the program, Bush staff rated only 50 percent of the programs as likely to be continued after the Bush support ceased. But colleges have gone out and raised endowment funds; state universities have obtained legislative or state board support; faculty development has achieved a status of high priority. Now, two years after the first estimate, the Bush staff estimates that all but two of the institutions will maintain a level of faculty development substantially above that they had funded prior to the Bush grant; in fact, four institutions expect to increase funding for faculty development even beyond the level added by the Bush grant.

Effects on Individual Faculty Members. We have already seen that large numbers of faculty members participated in Bush program activities and that 87 percent reported that their participation was productive. We have also seen that faculty *morale* and satisfaction with their roles was high.

Cognitive learning was also reported by faculty members as a result of the Bush program. A survey of Concordia College of Saint Paul taken before the Bush program was implemented revealed faculty frustration at the difficulty of keeping up with knowledge in their fields—a frustration reported by faculty at other colleges as well. Two years into the Bush program a resurvey revealed some decrease in this frustration. In answer to the open-ended question "What benefits do you feel you obtained from your participation?" 39 of the 100 respondents answering listed increased subject matter knowledge or improved course content. Six mentioned gaining a better understanding of the teaching-learning process. Nine mentioned learning about differences in student learning styles. Six mentioned greater understanding of student evaluations of teaching.

The Bush program appears to have resulted in changes in teaching. The reported improvement in teaching skills is particularly important because large numbers of faculty members saw this as the most important goal of the program. In response to the question "Did the program have an effect on teaching?" 78 percent of those who participated reported that they had made changes in their courses or teaching. Increases in teaching skill were frequent outcomes of participation (forty respondents). Participants reported such outcomes as increased skill in conducting discussions, better lecturing, improved ability to teach writing, and better skill in managing student time. One of the skills mentioned by those involved in writing workshops was improved skill in evaluating student work, the skill rated as the most important in a national survey of Canadian faculty members (Foster and Nelson, 1984).

While faculty members may sometimes be deluded about their own skill, it seems likely that, at the very least, these perceived changes in skill contribute to faculty members' enjoyment of teaching and, as we have argued earlier, enjoying teaching is one of the fundamentals in continued development of teachers. Not that we would discount these self-judgments of improved skill. Generally speaking, faculty members are relatively good judges of when they are teaching well or poorly (Marsh, 1982), and it seems probable that increases in faculty skill are likely to facilitate student learning.

We would have liked to have independent corroboration of changes in teaching. Two of our colleges provided data from student ratings, a potentially useful source even though the students have no opportunity to compare the faculty member's teaching before and after the Bush program experience, and overall ratings of all faculty members in the college not only include nonparticipants but are affected by many variables outside the specific outcomes of the Bush program. At both colleges, student ratings of teaching before the Bush program were relatively good. At Mary College the ratings remained about the same during the first two years of the program. At the College of Saint Teresa student ratings were higher after the Bush program was implemented.

Finally, 14 percent of the Bush program participant sample (and 33 percent of those serving on planning committees) reported that their participation had resulted in *publications.* Faculty members in the social sciences and humanities were more likely than those from the natural sciences or vocational areas to report publications resulting from their participation. Some of these were scholarly articles or books; others were discussions of educational or teaching issues related to Bush program activities.

Most Effective Types of Programs

An amazing diversity of programs were proposed and carried out by the Bush grantees. The most common aspect of the Bush programs was faculty grants, offered by two thirds of the grantee institutions. Ten colleges or universities carried out revisions of curricula, and ten gave grants for development of new courses (frequently interdisciplinary).

The twenty-four institutions who received grants carried out thirty-seven different types of programs as categorized in the first issue of *Plantings:*

1. Advising techniques
2. Career planning and professional development
3. Computer skills
4. Continuing program development
5. Course development and improvement
6. Curriculum revision
7. Department chairperson development
8. Department review and planning
9. Evaluation of teaching and learning
10. Faculty development centers (physical facility and materials)
11. Faculty exchange
12. Field visits to other campuses

13. Graduate degrees
14. Grants (for curriculum development, travel, and faculty development activities)
15. Individual professional development—research and advanced study
16. Interdisciplinary programs
17. Internships in nonacademic settings
18. Library search techniques and materials
19. New and junior faculty programs
20. Organizational development—governing systems
21. Outside lecturers and consultants
22. Overseas apprenticeships
23. Part-time faculty development
24. Proposal- and grant-writing techniques
25. Research related to faculty development
26. Retirement
27. Retraining for other fields
28. Sabbatical and other leave grants
29. Seminars on teaching and learning
30. Senior associate program—senior faculty working with new faculty
31. Student-assisted research
32. Student-faculty dialogues
33. Summer institutes
34. Teacher consultations—faculty helping faculty
35. Theories of excellence and creativity
36. Writing programs
37. Workshops on teaching and learning

We looked at the following sources of evidence of success:

1. Decision to end, or to add, a particular program
2. Number of participants
3. Satisfaction of participants
4. Impact of the program upon institution and faculty

Our data on effectiveness come primarily from our visits

to the campuses. In addition we obtained the progress reports of the institutions. In each institution with several types of programs, we asked the program director to rank their programs in terms of impact on students' learning, faculty learning and motivation, and the institution as a whole.

If we measure effectiveness by participation, *instructional development activities,* such as workshops, seminars, and lectures, were the most effective programs. In some institutions almost every faculty member had participated in at least one such event. Moreover, many of the significant outcomes mentioned in our overall evaluation resulted from such events. As indicated both in site visits and in responses to our questionnaires, changes in norms and communication patterns, for example, often developed out of common workshop experiences. As one faculty member said, "I found that I met faculty members in other departments who use discussion and now compare experiences with them." On several campuses, increased mention of student learning styles in faculty conversation resulted from workshops on William Perry's theory of development in college students. The effects of workshops were not restricted to faculty members. Program directors ranked workshops high in terms of the workshops' impact on student learning.

Writing across the curriculum was one of the most frequently offered projects and was rated the most effective by program directors. One fact supporting this judgment is that colleges maintained or expanded this program in their renewal requests. For example, the Minnesota State University system asked for increased support for this activity in its renewal application, and Augsburg added a writing project in its renewal applications. Public schools that had participated in the Dakota Writing Project workshops paid for additional workshops for other teachers. In applying for a renewal, officials of the Minnesota State University system reported that participants in writing projects were more likely to make changes in their courses and teaching than participants in other projects. Faculty members at several campuses reported that student writing had improved after writing programs began, and almost invariably faculty participants recognized improvement in their own writing.

The success of writing programs seems to rest upon a number of factors:

- The writing workshops helped faculty members develop skills enabling them to do a better job without a major increase in time. For example, the writing workshops taught faculty members how to provide better feedback to students without greater time spent grading papers through such techniques as the use of short papers, multiple drafts, and peer evaluation.
- In learning to teach writing, faculty members not only gained greater self-competence in teaching but also gained writing competence themselves.
- Working to learn how to improve student writing had spillover effects in faculty thinking about the goals of education and in classroom teaching methods. Lectures were broken up for short periods of writing; faculty members encouraged more student activity in learning and thinking.
- The writing program facilitated interaction and cooperation across disciplinary boundaries.

Workshops on teaching writing were mentioned not only as a source of new teaching skill but also as developing new norms about expectations of student writing.

If one wants to change norms, it is tempting to require all faculty members to attend relevant workshops, seminars, or lectures. In fact, however, faculty members (like students) tended to be less enthusiastic about those activities that were required.

Projects involving *course development* and *curricular change* were also rated as highly productive by our faculty respondents. Moreover, the three colleges whose programs were most successful in terms of a composite of our criteria all employed curricular change. Program directors rated their course development and curricular change programs high in terms of their impact on student learning, faculty motivation, and the institution as a whole. Although ratings of *professional growth* programs were favorable, they were slightly lower (3.2) than those for curricular change (3.4) and instructional development

(3.3). (A rating of 3 = moderately productive; 4 = very productive.) Professional development grants would be presumed to be of most direct personal benefit to the faculty members who received them, as compared with curricular change or instructional development activities, and faculty members did value grants —but not as much as curricular change, which seems to be primarily of value to the institution.

As we saw earlier, when faculty members are asked what faculty development efforts they would like to have, professional growth programs involving grants for faculty members are usually rated highest. Sabbatical supplements, stipends for summer research or instructional development, and grants for travel to professional meetings were features of several Bush programs that were valued by participants. There is the danger, however, that grant programs will exacerbate envy among those not receiving grants. While we do not have direct evidence about this, nineteen of our respondents wrote that the Bush program primarily benefited researchers; these respondents were mostly at institutions providing grants for scholarly activities.

Grant programs are unlikely to affect norms unless a purposeful effort is made to use the grants as catalysts for institutional change through faculty forums, newsletters, and follow-up activities drawing upon the experience of the grantees and relating their learning to the interests and needs of other faculty members. In one institution, which made a laudable effort to have grantees speak about their grant activities, the narrow, technical nature of some projects led to diminishing interest and lagging attendance. Our impression is that the degree to which faculty grants eventually affected teaching and learning was related to the degree to which a faculty development committee or officer consulted with grantees about teaching and the relevance of the grant to teaching. Rather than simply screening proposals, some committees or administrators overseeing grants took strongly proactive stances to emphasize relationships to teaching.

One side benefit of faculty grants programs is their value for the faculty development committee (or other grant-giving committee). Members of these committees worked hard, but in the process, they were forced to communicate their ideas about educational and scholarly values to their fellow committee members. They learned about the interests and aspirations of colleagues across the disciplines, and they gained a greater sense of identification with their institution.

Several institutions made grants for projects involving students working with faculty members on research. Although the numbers of faculty and students involved were small, the testimonials of the students and faculty members involved were favorable. The impact on the learning of a small number of students was direct and convincingly presented. Neither in these nor in other Bush programs, however, have faculty been very ingenious in involving students in their activities. While the success of such faculty-student links depends to some extent upon a match in interest, personality, and expectations between students and faculty, some of the seemingly most successful arrangements involved small groups of students rather than a simple one-to-one apprenticeship.

What kinds of institutions were most successful? One of the impressive conclusions from our visits to the campuses and our analysis of the data was that there were no real failures among the programs. Although some seemed to us to be more successful than others, there was no instance in which we came away with the feeling "That grant was a waste of money."

Overall, our results support the conclusion that the Bush grants had the greatest impact on the smaller, less prestigious, less affluent institutions. After the fact, such a finding seems obvious, but it did not seem so obvious when the grant proposals came in. Correlations between the ratings of the original proposals and of ratings of success as of 1983 were low. Some of those institutions who implemented successful programs had difficulty in writing proposals that communicated their ability to carry out good programs. Their plans often seemed less innovative and less realistic than those of other applicants; their ability to release staff time, to provide adequate leadership seemed more dubious. It is a tribute both to the colleges and to the Bush staff and consultants, who worked with them, that viable programs emerged.

Our theoretical discussion of faculty development in the introductory chapters stressed the importance of faculty norms in establishing standards of excellence in education. It is here where the Bush programs show especial impact upon the smaller colleges. In many of these colleges, almost every member of the faculty was involved in at least one of the Bush program activities. Faculty members in small colleges were particularly cognizant of changes in norms. In colleges with fewer than 1,000 students, sixteen out of eighteen faculty respondents perceived a change in norms; in colleges with between 1,000 and 1,999 students, twenty-five perceived a change in norms, eighteen did not. In colleges with between 2,000 and 5,000 students, thirty-five faculty respondents noted a change in norms, ten did not; in public institutions, thirty perceived a change, fifteen did not.

Faculty members in the middle-sized colleges (1,000–5,000) were most likely to feel that the Bush program had had a significant effect upon communication. We interpret this as indicating that it is more difficult to effect such changes in the large colleges and that in the smallest colleges, "communication was already good," as one respondent wrote.

Although the difficulty of influencing the direction or velocity of any great mass is probably as great with institutional as with physical objects, we were, nevertheless, highly impressed with the success of the Bush programs in several larger institutions. As we saw in Chapter Eight, the University of North Dakota carried out a range of diverse activities that met a number of needs of the university and its faculty. Similarly, the institutions in the Minnesota State University system were successful in achieving unusual cooperation among state-level administrators, university vice-presidents, and faculty members at a diverse group of institutions. Their writing program used existing faculty expertise to train and assist faculty members at their own and other institutions in the system.

In addition to classifying institutions by size, we also tried another way of classifying institutions—breaking them into three groups: the large universities, the colleges emphasizing traditional liberal arts, and the colleges and smaller state universities with large proportions of students in vocationally oriented programs, such as nursing, education, or business. This grouping revealed that the Bush program was particularly successful in the vocationally oriented colleges, both in terms of affecting collegiate norms and in faculty satisfaction with their role.

We also classified institutions in terms of selectivity based on mean Scholastic Aptitude Test or American College Testing Program scores. No differences in program effectiveness emerged.

What kinds of programs were effective in particular kinds of institutions? Our overall judgment in answer to this question is that colleges and universities are pretty good judges of their own needs. Thus what each institution proposed did, in our judgment, serve the needs of that institution quite well. As mentioned earlier, the original proposals often were poked and prodded a good deal by the Bush Foundation staff and consultants before the grant was made, so that we cannot conclude that foundations could simply give funds to colleges and let them do what seemed best. And of course we have no way of assessing what might have happened if Carleton College and the University of Minnesota had emphasized workshops rather than faculty grants or if Bethel College and the Dakota Writing Project had given grants for scholarly research rather than carrying out projects to teach writing.

As we saw earlier in this chapter, grant programs are high on the faculty list of preferences for faculty development funds, and faculty members at Carleton and Minnesota were enthusiastic about the positive effects of their grant programs not only for the recipients but for morale generally. Such an outcome is not inevitable. Since no program is able to make grants to every faculty member, a grant program has the potential to create tensions between grant recipients and nonrecipients.

The potential impact of the two grant programs upon the entire faculty can be seen by the fact that over a third of the Carleton faculty received large or small grants in the first two years of the program, a proportion much harder to achieve in a very large university. At Carleton, the grant program helped restore and strengthen faculty members' self-perceptions as contributing members of the community of scholars. At the University of Minnesota the grants helped direct attention to the value of undergraduate teaching and reduce perceived imbalance between research and teaching.

Not only did the grants have a positive effect upon current faculty members, but the program also had a favorable impact upon faculty recruiting according to a Carleton administrator, a testimonial supported by other colleges.

As we saw in Chapter Five, the smallest colleges seem to have the greatest need for programs providing basic help for faculty members to increase or broaden subject matter and teaching competence, for travel to professional meetings, and for opportunities to upgrade courses and curricula. Thus while both the larger or more prestigious institutions and the smaller colleges emphasized professional development programs, the link to curricular needs was much closer in the smaller schools.

Factors Influencing Faculty Development Program Success

In Chapter Two, we proposed five hypotheses. We now look at the evidence supporting, or failing to support, those hypotheses.

Faculty Ownership. We suggested that programs would be more effective if faculty members felt that the program was *their* program. Our measures of faculty ownership are indirect. One was a rating of the Bush staff with respect to the degree to which faculty or administration took the initiative in planning the program. A second was the response of our random sample of faculty to the question "How much input do you feel faculty have had into these programs at your college?" A third was the question "How much input do you feel you have had into the faculty development program?"

Relating these measures to our various outcome measures, we found that those institutions in which there was balanced faculty-administration planning were significantly more successful than those where administration dominated or where faculty dominated. Our faculty respondents' ratings of amount of faculty input was positively correlated with most criteria of success. A greater sense of faculty input was correlated (.43) with perceived changes in faculty norms. The respondents' own feeling of having input was highly correlated across institutions with the amount of faculty participation in programs and with mean faculty satisfaction.

Administrative Support. Our second hypothesis was that effective programs require strong administrative support. Part of our evidence comes from our site visits. Nothing we saw disproved this hypothesis. Obviously, every site visit included a visit with administrators who were uniformly enthusiastic about the value of the Bush program. Nonetheless, there were some variations in the degree of operational support given by administrators; in responses to our questionnaires, faculty perceptions of administrative support were positively related to faculty satisfaction.

Optimally, the administration is supportive, even directive, without being intrusive. In some cases, key leadership was provided by effective, respected faculty members; in other cases, a dean or associate dean carried major responsibility. It is almost tautological to conclude that the success of the program depended as much upon the effectiveness of the leadership as upon the objective characteristics of the programs offered. But we observed instances where programs faltered when key administrators or faculty leaders left, changed roles, or had to devote their energies to crises or other pressing activities.

Local Expertise Versus Outside Consultants. We had hypothesized greater success with local expertise, but on this hypothesis we guessed wrong. Not every outside consultant was a great success, but the majority seem, both from our site visit observations and from our questionnaire responses, to have provided valuable stimulation and insights. Particularly successful were the Minnesota State University system's use of outside consultants for departmental reviews and the workshops given at several colleges using William Perry's categorization of student learning styles.

The most common, and probably most successful, use of local talent was in computer expertise. A number of colleges either used their own computer experts or sent faculty members for training needed to instruct the rest of the faculty in computer uses in academia. The success of this use of local faculty as contrasted with the less conspicuous success of local teaching consultants, master teachers, mentors, and so on, can probably be accounted for by one principle. Faculty members, like other human beings, are reluctant to admit incompetence in their regular work. Thus faculty members are not likely to seek help from a colleague on normal teaching skills. Computers, however, are new—outside the realm of typical teaching activities. To seek to learn something about computers is thus not a threat to one's self-esteem or reputation. In fact, it may rather be credited as contributing to one's self and public image as intellectually curious, a continuing learner.

Follow-Up Activities. Some one-shot programs seem to have been effective in stimulating continuing effects, but on the whole, we were convinced that follow-up meetings, refresher training, public reports to the faculty, and so on were good investments in increasing the likelihood of lasting impact.

Faculty Preferences. When faculty members are asked how funds for faculty development should be spent, they typically (as reported in national surveys) rate sabbatical supplements, summer research support, released time, and travel most highly. As we saw in our comparisons of the results of programs for professional development, instructional development, and curricular change, our analysis suggests that even though grants for individual scholarly activities are valued, curricular change, workshops, and other programs involving faculty members working together to achieve common objectives may be more cost-effective for the institution in terms of their impact on student learning.

Conclusions

The overall message of this chapter is positive. Faculty development programs can be evaluated and can make a difference. The difficulties of making an evaluation, particularly that of producing quantitative data, should not preclude seeking and using a wide variety of information. Nor should the difficulty of evaluation preclude the initiating of faculty development activities. Information can come from the faculty and administrators affected as well as from outside observers. Site visits and interviews are useful as well as questionnaires addressed to elicit specific information and to assess outcomes. Evaluation efforts, like those made for the Bush program, can have useful formative as well as summative effects. Though individual program evaluation was a weakness within this program, evaluation efforts were carried out by all institutions. The evaluation procedures used in this study clearly indicate that faculty development programs can make a difference. Our findings with respect to these differences are in the final chapter.

❧ 11 ❧

Looking Ahead:
Establishing Faculty
Development Programs
to Improve
Undergraduate Education

At this writing, November 1984, about two thirds of the colleges and universities in the Bush Foundation Faculty Development Program have finished their first three years of activity. The remainder roughly divide into those with two years experience and those whose programs are a year old or just under way. Most of those that have completed the first grant have been given renewal grants for three additional years, after which Bush funding will end. At that time, a more complete assessment can be made of the impact of the programs. Only then can that pragmatic test be precisely applied: Did these programs so declare their worth that they are being substantially maintained by institutional funds?

At this time, it appears that the institutions have taken the steps necessary to meet that criterion. As we saw earlier, institutions have already increased their own budgetary commitments and have raised earmarked endowment funds; public institutions are building faculty development into their continuing state budgets. All except two of the institutions appear to

207

be confident of at least maintaining the faculty development programs stimulated by the Bush grants—a substantial increase from the pre-Bush levels.

In preparing this report, we queried the other major foundations that have made faculty development grants and studied the outcomes of their programs. These earlier and continuing activities achieved important goals, but none seems to have achieved the level of success we found in the Bush Faculty Development Program. How can one account for this success? No doubt the times increase the need for faculty development. Nonetheless, we suspect that a key factor was that the presidents of private colleges and the University of Minnesota were partially responsible for initiation of the program. Their assertions that faculty development held high priority among their needs not only supported the Bush Foundation's own analysis but guaranteed that the program had strong administrative support—a factor not as often true for the earlier foundation and federally supported faculty development programs.

But there is a danger in strong administrative support. A faculty development program may be perceived by faculty as an indication that the administration thinks the faculty is so inadequate that it needs special help to improve. Here the Bush Foundation's strong pressure to involve faculty in planning paid off. On almost every campus we found a strong sense of faculty involvement and ownership. The programs were *college* programs, not *administration* or *faculty development committee* programs. Those affected by the programs were collaborators rather than targets. The fact that the Bush Foundation valued the college and its proposal enough to invest a substantial amount of money was in itself a source of encouragement and reinforcement for that college community, perhaps even more than if the same program had been funded from institutional funds.

The conclusions in this chapter are based on the data and observations in the separate chapters. The renewal proposals we have seen support our assumptions arrived at from recent site visits and institutional reports of the first cycle of grants. Programs will continue much as we have described them here and with a high possibility of continuing results.

Although our observations specifically apply to the institutions in the Bush program, they obviously apply to other institutions of a similar kind. The last part of this chapter will stress these applications.

Planning

What characterized the successful Bush programs? After-the-fact judgments may be dubious, but it appears to us that the most successful programs were ones that were especially careful and complete in their planning. Faculty members were involved. There was broad consultation between faculty and administration so that both faculty and administrators understood what was planned and what was necessary to carry out the plans. These proposals generally were characterized by a clear sense of purpose.

Nine institutions received planning grants to help them shape proposals. This appears to have been money well spent, and for the following reasons. The objectives and methods of faculty development are not clearly understood. Colleges and universities at any given time are aware of needs that affect faculty performance and student learning, but few have arrived at the point of identifying and giving priority to needs that can help shape a program. Cooperation of faculty and administration and arousing interest and enthusiasm are vital to faculty development programs; the coming together of faculty and administrators in the planning process helps create both. At many colleges and universities, the support given through a planning grant enables individuals to give time to planning that would not be easily forthcoming otherwise. A consistent response by a majority of faculty in their responses to our questionnaire was that of having too much to do. In addition, perspectives gained through a planning grant in the give-and-take between the institution and the foundation staff and consultants are useful. As these programs have developed, institutions with little experience in making proposals of this kind have examples close at hand helpful to their own planning.

Whether planning grants are available or not, a firm conclusion from this study is that faculty development programs need to be shaped by the individual college or university and be invested with a sense of faculty ownership. The importance of strong faculty participation in planning is obvious. While the experience with faculty development in this study adds to an accumulating body of experience useful to planning individual programs, it has not provided templates for ready-made institutional programs. Nor is it the conclusion of this study that proceeding as if there were such sure patterns is a wise procedure. In short, planning may well be considered an important part of the program itself.

A related matter is that these institutions varied considerably as to who was most responsible for originating the plan. For by far the greatest number, the faculty provided the strongest impulse behind the plan and remained central in shaping the proposal and in administering its activities. The administration played a larger part in a small number of proposals, and faculty and administrators were judged to have struck a balance in about the same number. Each of these rough groupings, it should be noted, included successful programs, emphasizing the point that successful planning may be more a matter of getting it done than of who provides the originating impulse. But administrative participation is also important. A balanced administration-faculty planning effort resulted in greater success (as measured by the sum of our criteria) than either administration-dominated or faculty-dominated planning.

Some common weaknesses in planning observed in this study are in (1) sorting out what most needs doing and what might best be accomplished, (2) examining closely relationships between faculty activities and student learning, (3) considering impact of program both on individual faculty and instructional effectiveness at large, and (4) carefully considering evaluation possibilities and procedures. Laundry lists of needs are a common first approach to a proposal. Sorting out is not only a matter of identifying realizable priorities but of more sharply identifying educational aims and institutional capabilities. Identifying the linkage between faculty performance and student learning is still the most elusive aspect of this study; difficult as it is, it is both necessary to campus planning and probably more amenable to close scrutiny on an individual campus. So, too, an individual college can best consider how the various aspects of a program might be expected to affect, with some degree of specificity, the academic program at large and even the general climate for learning. Program evaluation of any kind is difficult; without clearly specifying what and how evaluation is to be made, results fall short even of those evaluations in which what is proposed is not carried out.

A final conclusion about planning is really a number of cautions arising from tracing program features back to planning activities. Some programs reflected less of a consensus than of yielding to strongly held individual ideas and convictions. Whether these come from administrators or faculty, they can saddle a program with features having little appeal to, or effect upon, large numbers of faculty and can increase the ever-present possibility of a scatter-gun program that has little collective impact. A number of programs seem unduly affected by the appeal of one or another of the recurrent theories or methodologies that move in, and most often out, of education. The polite acceptance of such ideas in the planning may well lead to reluctant carrying out in the actual program.

Administration

It is difficult to describe just what constitutes effective leadership. Like effective teachers, effective leaders come in all sizes and shapes, and have different styles and different ways of getting their way and helping others get theirs. But clearly within these programs, the presence of individual faculty and administrative leadership was important to a program's success. Where there was little leadership, programs faltered. Where there was imposition of authority or convictions masquerading as leadership, programs had difficulty in getting off the ground.

The shaping of proposals in the first place called upon leadership, usually from an academic vice-president or president. In most instances, it also called for an early identifying of faculty leadership and some relinquishing of a primary role to that individual or individuals. In the ideal instance, faculty leadership succeeded in gaining general faculty support and enthusiasm, kept a working group of faculty at their necessary tasks, and worked with the confidence that comes from strong backing by administrators and the kind of administrative support they can provide. At the opposite extreme, and in few instances in this study, academic administrators were unable to find the faculty leadership that could give energy and coherence to a proposal. Reluctant to impose their own authority or imposing such authority at the price of arousing strong faculty resistance, some few administrators did not provide the kind of leadership successful programs depend upon.

Judging from these programs, one can only conclude that leadership capacities are not lacking even among small aggregations of faculty and administrators. The only qualifications that need be made are that at small institutions these resources, as well as those of other kinds, may be spread thin and at large institutions the magnitude and diversity of the academic program may call upon extraordinary leadership capacities. We observed in a number of instances how the presence of specific individuals made a crucial difference in a program and, conversely, how the absence of such an individual by a shift in assignment or leaving for another position consequentially affected a program. We also observed the problem in a large university of giving faculty development the magnitude and visibility that might affect the academic program at large. Within the large institutions, we saw enough of a range of leadership at all academic levels and within the faculty to suggest that even among large institutions, individual actions can still count.

Aside from the obvious needs of sustaining a program's impact and managing its details, leaders in faculty development programs can well extend their capacities in the interest of harmonizing faculty development efforts with institutional practices and policies. Reward systems, for example, have an effect upon faculty performance even though faculty tend to be intrinsically more than extrinsically motivated. A number of programs within our sample raised questions about whether faculty energies given to program-supported activities would be recognized within the reward system. One university's program was engaged in working with appropriate faculty committees on this specific question. Faculty development programs may have an unintended impact in bringing more faculty into exercising leadership that can beneficially affect institutional practices and policies.

Administrative and faculty leadership may be most crucial in continuing programs beyond the period of Bush Foundation support. One aspect is that of fund raising, apparent among the number of presidents who are attempting to raise specific endowments for faculty development or to incorporate such endowments into capital fund drives. But a supporting kind of leadership can come from both faculty and administrators in arguing for the worth of faculty development programs among intensely competing priorities.

Program Activities

As shown in our analyses in Chapter Ten, curriculum change and instructional development emerged as more successful than we had expected, and faculty grants, while useful, seemed to be less cost-effective in terms of impact upon education. The differences between our results and those of earlier investigators such as Siegel (1980) may be a function of different times, different investigators, or different measures of success. In any case, all three activities produced good results.

Workshops, particularly, seem to have been much more successful in our institutions than in those studied by Nelsen and Siegel (1980). We suspect that this was partly a result of effective involvement of faculty in planning, partly a result of choice of workshop leaders, and partly a result of the choice of topics. Such topics as teaching writing and computer uses in higher education are current interests of faculty members and, as we saw earlier, offer value to the faculty member personally, as well as to the faculty members' teaching. But more conventional topics, such as student learning styles and teaching by discussion, were also viewed as successful by our respondents. Foster and Nelson (1984) found in their national surveys of Canadian faculty members a strongly perceived need for help in evaluating student performance and discussion techniques, such as asking questions. It may well be that faculty attitudes toward workshops are becoming more favorable.

Curriculum projects, our highest-rated activity, were not inevitably successful, especially when the impetus for change came primarily from an administrator. But when faculty and administration jointly were committed to reexamination, the resulting process of reexamination of goals and teaching methods seemed often to result in heightened morale, improved communication, a greater sense of community, and a strengthened commitment to excellence. Writing across the curriculum was one of the most frequent program elements, and despite some variation in the means by which faculty training was carried out, the results were substantially positive in all cases. Success was due not only to the importance of effective writing as an educational goal but also because the process involved activities cutting across disciplinary lines involving faculty members in groups with shared goals.

A leading question for any institution is whether a *single-focus* or a *cafeteria* program will produce the best results. Our general answer to this question is a caution to avoid both extremes. Single-focus programs were a distinct minority among the Bush programs, and none of them rated as high in our evaluation as programs that sponsored a variety of faculty development activities. On the other hand, we did not give high marks to programs that offered a smorgasbord of activities with little attention to how one part might reinforce another or how all the parts were related to a common purpose.

Impact

As indicated in the preceding chapter, we proceeded in our evaluation with the intention of tracing the Bush Faculty Development Program success from the initial response of the institutions in writing proposals, through the carrying out of the activities proposed, to the impact upon college norms, faculty morale, and faculty teaching practices. We had strong hopes that for at least some programs we would be able to follow the path to its ultimate end—impact upon student learning. In this effort we were not very successful. We do have in two instances evidence from student ratings of teaching, but we do not have measures of actual changes in student achievement measures of course goals. Nonetheless, the number of converging sources of evidence is so impressive that we would be willing to place bets on the generalization that the program did have a favorable impact upon student learning in almost every, or perhaps every, institution receiving a grant.

One piece of evidence confirming our judgment is that the institutions are making similar bets. As we have seen, some hard-headed administrators and trustees have been so impressed by the results of the activities supported by the Bush program that they have dedicated future budgets to continuation of faculty development activities. In these times of endemic cuts in budgets, the priority these institutions are willing to place on faculty development is perhaps the ultimate test of the perceived value of the Bush program activities.

Whatever the impact upon other outcomes, one lasting impact is clear, and that is the impact upon concepts of faculty development and the support given to it. As Robert Young, director of faculty development at the University of North Dakota, pointed out after a consultation visit to one of our colleges, prior to the Bush program, faculty development was viewed by many faculty and administrators in the traditional terms of sabbatical leaves for scholarly activities. Now in every institution the view extends much further, to include a wider variety of possibilities for faculty learning about teaching methods, student characteristics, and theories of learning and problem solving as well as development as teachers, advisers, and participants in group activities.

One of our major conclusions is that in terms of cost-effectiveness, the Bush program grants had the greatest impact per dollar upon the smaller institutions. As our data indicate, the smaller colleges involved a greater proportion of their faculty members in Bush program activities; they reported greater changes in norms about teaching than did the larger institutions, and in some cases, according to the judgments of the site visitors, the grants made significant changes in the climate of hope versus depression accompanying the severe financial problems that some of the smaller institutions were having. This is not to imply that the grants to the larger institutions were without value, but it is obviously much harder to have an impact upon the total institution in a university of the size of the University of Minnesota as compared with a college the size of Dakota Wesleyan University or the College of Saint Teresa.

Future Directions

Advice to Administrators and Faculty Development Committees. At one of our discussions, each of the evaluators and Bush Foundation staff informally identified his own choices of most and least successful programs. We will not identify these choices, which have little claim to precision of judgment, but will observe that a degree of unanimity was to be found at each end of the scale. What is more useful is the discussion that followed in which we identified features of programs that led to our judgments. Most of these, as should be apparent, have been discussed in previous sections of this chapter.

Of the most successful programs, these characteristics were singled out:

- They were careful and complete in their planning.
- They offered neither too extensive a cafeteria nor were too focused on limited objectives. The diversity of opportunities recognized a diversity of faculty needs and interests but still maintained a program identity.
- They had effective leadership from both faculty and administrators without diminishing the feeling of faculty ownership of the program.
- They enlisted substantial numbers of faculty in planning and administering the program; the institution and the program were well suited to one another.
- They were not initiated in ways that threatened the faculty or increased insecurity.
- They did not aim at "deadwood" or "developing" those who

had been ineffective but rather offered opportunities for the solid, substantial contributors as well as the "stars" or the alienated; they gave the faculty a sense that they were valued.

- They stimulated faculty enthusiasm and a high rate of participation of the faculty in various aspects of the program.
- They created situations in which faculty members felt increased colleague support for investments in teaching and a greater sense that administrators valued teaching.
- They had a visibility on campus among faculty and, to some degree, among students, beyond being known to those who directly benefited from the program.
- They took account of time pressure, inviting greater investment but not demanding permanent additions to the faculty work load.
- The activities of the program resulted in tangible changes in courses, teaching strategies, subject matter competence, curricula and the like from which reasonable inferences could be made as to improving student learning.
- They provided training to develop new skills, not just exhortation.
- The activities increased interaction and communication among faculty and students in working toward common goals. At the highest degree of success, the program created a better climate for teaching and learning; commitment to teaching and communicating about teaching became normative.
- The program took risks; it challenged the faculty to stretch individual efforts and to see beyond their own professional growth toward its impact on both students and the institution.

The list of characteristics of least successful programs is shorter, as it should be, in reflecting the general success of the Bush programs:

- They were well planned and carried out but served chiefly limited or routine interests of the faculty and administration.

- They lacked a sense of purpose, particularly as they might carry out the aims of enhancing student learning, which was the underlying objective of the Bush project.
- They failed to arouse faculty enthusiasm or to bring forth effective leadership from either faculty or administration.
- They recognized specific problems that faculty development might have helped meet, but they did not propose or pursue appropriate or effective strategies.

Advice to Foundations. For the Bush Foundation staff, the ultimate question is not only was this money well spent but also could it have paid off more fully if spent in some other way. Making the assumption that the Foundation's goal was to improve undergraduate education, we can think of no alternatives that seem likely to have a bigger payoff. The Foundation might, for example, simply have given grants to each college to use for whatever needs had highest priority, but this alternative dims in appeal when one examines the impact of the planning activities, the considerable help given by Bush staff and consultants, and the effect of a major grant aimed at improving undergraduate education through faculty development in focusing attention and energy on educational purposes. We believe that neither nonrestricted grants to the institutions nor grants restricted to other purposes would have generated as much productive faculty activity as this program.

Since our overall evaluation of the Bush program is favorable, it is natural to ask what to do next. We offer several alternatives, not necessarily incompatible. One obvious answer is to extend it to other regions. The results to date have such high promise that further investments in extending, refining, and improving seem justified. While one might not predict similar payoff for a faithful replication region by region, the results of our evaluation strengthen the case for increasing the investment in similar programs, making use of the lessons learned in this program.

We see a number of other areas where faculty development activities might also play an important role in improving the quality of education. From our analyses of results so far, we see grants for *curriculum study* and revision as a particularly valuable investment for the future of higher education. We have already discussed the advantages of curricular change for faculty development—its effect upon communication and institutional norms, its ability to address problems of teaching and educational aims without the threat to self-esteem involved in direct attacks upon poor teaching, and its ability to involve faculty members who need revitalization but avoid conventional faculty development activities. Here we would like to argue that aside from its indirect value for faculty development, curriculum change is timely in itself. Faculty concern about the relationship between liberal education and vocational education surfaced in many of our site visits; increased attention to basic skills in reading, writing, and mathematics is reflected not only in the programs for writing across the curriculum but also in debates about the role of remedial education in colleges and universities; the almost omnipresent microcomputer still remains a question mark so far as its having a role in teaching and the curriculum; numerous colleges have taken computer literacy (whatever it may be) as an educational goal coordinate with verbal literacy.

At the same time, theoretical and scholarly progress in the disciplines and among disciplines suggests the need for rethinking the structure and sequencing of the curriculum, and new developments in cognitive science offer hope for a better understanding of how the curriculum can influence lifelong learning and thinking. "New" students, entering with diverse backgrounds and goals, also question conventional curricular structures. The modest revisions of the Harvard curriculum represented an early approach to this problem; the curricular change projects in the Bush Faculty Development Program are, we believe, precursors of continuing rethinking of the curriculum throughout American higher education.

Another obvious possibility for the future is to extend the Bush Faculty Development Program to community colleges. While many community college faculty members have had training in pedagogical techniques as part of their undergraduate or graduate education, the role of the community college teacher is one that sometimes limits professional development. Most community college teachers, like their peers in the four-year colleges, are intellectually curious, intelligent—intrinsically motivated—but their teaching situation limits the ability to satisfy these motives. Community college teachers have little opportunity to offer specialized courses in the areas of their interests; teaching loads tend to be heavier; and there is less opportunity to work closely with individual students and follow their development over an extended period of time. There is the danger that teaching becomes a forty-hour-a-week job in which one simply meets classes, corrects papers, and makes teaching and learning as dull as dish washing. The problem of faculty development is different from that in four-year institutions in terms of the need to help faculty members maintain enthusiasm despite teaching assignments involving repetitious teaching of the same course. Our experience in working with community college teachers has been that they enjoy teaching and welcome opportunities to learn about teaching—so faculty development efforts in community colleges fall upon fertile soil.

Complicating the problem, however, is that many community college faculty members are part-time. A Bush program directed at part-time faculty members, not only in community colleges but in the four-year institutions, could have a significant impact upon education.

A similar problem exists in the graduate institutions that use graduate student teaching assistants for large portions of instruction in lower-level courses. Probably the most complaints about quality of teaching in the large universities are directed at teaching by untrained and unsupervised graduate student teaching assistants. There is ample evidence that teaching assistants can perform a valid educational function when properly supervised and trained, so that grants directed toward the development of such programs could be of much value. Training in basic skills in questioning, leading discussions, and grading papers can be helpful.

For any of these areas, we believe that some of our findings would be useful in shaping new programs. For example, the importance of local planning and of faculty commitment is likely to prove equally as important in the development of the new programs we have suggested as it was in those we have evaluated. Similarly, the importance of institutions thinking about new and better ways of achieving their goals rather than simply supporting their traditional approaches seems likely to yield better cost-effectiveness.

Our final suggestion for future directions for funding may represent an admission of failure on our part. It is that the Bush Foundation or other agencies interested in faculty development and undergraduate education fund detailed analytic evaluations of particular program activities such as writing across the curriculum, curricular revision programs, or faculty grant activities. Our aspirations were to have done that in this project, but we succeeded only in very general respects. We still do not know what kinds of training programs in teaching writing have what kinds of effects upon the skills of faculty outside English departments; we still do not know what inhibits faculty members from participating in such programs; we still do not know what the impact of such programs is, not only upon specific kinds and aspects of student writing but also upon students' attitudes toward writing and their understanding of the processes they use in writing. Evaluating writing has become increasingly sophisticated (White, 1985); the means for evaluating the impact of writing programs appears to be at hand. We would like to see such evaluations carried out for a number of types of faculty development activities.

Faculty Development in 1985–2000. What about the faculty of the future? In the late 1990s we will see an upswing in faculty hiring as retirements of the current aging faculty begin to reach large numbers. What kinds of programs will be needed for these newcomers to the academic profession? Our present data do not yield strong indicators, since the overwhelming majority of our faculties were experienced, tenured individuals. Nonetheless, we have arrived at some strongly felt conclusions about the nature of younger faculty members' needs:

1. Younger faculty members feel severe time pressures. Thus programs that give younger faculty members opportunities

to begin their teaching with a slightly reduced load, providing opportunities to plan courses in more detail and to get established in scholarly work are likely to be valuable. Yet such opportunities need to take account of departmental teaching needs. As we saw in two of our programs, young faculty members fear the blessing of a Bush grant will boomerang if it shifts greater teaching burdens onto their colleagues.

2. Young faculty members should probably not be engaged in developing major efforts to change their courses radically, such as by introducing Personalized System of Instruction, Guided Design, or some other effort requiring a great deal of time for planning and developing materials. Rather, young faculty members need to be given help in developing basic skills in test construction, conducting discussions, lecturing, and providing feedback to students through comments on papers.

3. Young faculty members need a sense of support from their peers; thus activities involving the development of communication and cooperation among younger faculty members are likely to be valuable. Just as valuable are efforts to increase communication about teaching and learning between young and experienced teachers.

Changing conditions are also likely to create specific needs in all members of the faculty. Two of these can be met by:

1. Continuing to increase the understanding of "new students" and "nontraditional students," as Patricia Cross has labeled the groups now underrepresented in higher education (Cross, 1980). With few exceptions, colleges and universities are now, more than ever, recruiting students more vigorously—at times with a vigor approaching that formerly used only to recruit football and basketball players. Faculty members still come predominantly from the ranks of bright, middle-class, academically motivated students. They have little experience in interacting with those of different

cultural backgrounds, motivation, and academic background. Simply having doctoral-level training in the substantive areas of a scholarly discipline will be insufficient to guarantee success in teaching a more diverse student population.

2. Learning how to teach nontraditional students more effectively can be related to learning to teach in nontraditional modes. As colleges increase their offerings of elderhostel programs, weekend colleges, distance courses, computer conferencing, and other nontraditional ways of meeting educational needs, it is likely that more faculty members will be doing more teaching in these settings. Typically such programs require more sophisticated advance planning and greater attention to student motivation and background than the teaching assignment of a standard required introductory course.

The effectiveness of higher education depends ultimately upon the faculty. As we have seen in the responses of the faculty members in our study, college teaching is a deeply satisfying career. We believe that faculty development programs not only enhance student learning but also can maintain and increase the satisfactions of teaching and of belonging to a community of learners.

Appendix

Questionnaire Submitted
to Selected Faculty at
Participating Institutions

As our letter introducing the survey indicated, we are obtaining information on faculty members' opinions about and experiences with the Bush Faculty Development Program at your institution. This information will help us provide the Bush Foundation with an overall evaluation of their program of grants. It is not an evaluation of your own institution's grant.

It is important to us that you answer each question, even those that may seem unimportant to you. We appreciate your willingness to participate.

For our part, we will keep your responses confidential. Data will be reported in aggregate form. The interview is voluntary, and should you come to any question that you do not wish to answer, go on to the next question. We hope that thinking about the issues of faculty development will be interesting and helpful to you as well as to us.

First, we would like to ask you about your knowledge of the Bush Faculty Development Program at your college.

1.   Are you aware of the program that is funded   *Yes*   *No*
     at your college?   1   2

     IF *NO,* GO TO QUESTION 19

2.   Do you have little, some, considerable, or a great deal of
     information about the program? (Circle your answer.)

3.   How did you find out about the program?

     _____
     _____
     _____
     _____

4a. Do you know any colleagues who have   *Yes*   *No*
     grants?   1   2

     IF *YES,* GO TO QUESTION 4b

4b. What are they doing with their grant(s)?

     _____
     _____
     _____
     _____

Now we would like to ask you about the goals of the program.

5.   What do you see as being the most important goals of
     the program?

     _____
     _____
     _____
     _____

6. How much input do you feel faculty members have had into these programs at your college (do you feel they have had little, some, considerable, or a great deal of input)? (Circle your answer.)

7. How much input do you feel you have had into the faculty development program (do you feel you have had little, some, considerable, or a great deal of input)? Circle your answer.)

8. Were you a member of the planning commit- *Yes No*
   tee?   1   2

9. What faculty groups benefit most from the program at this college?

   _____

   _____

   _____

   _____

10. Have you participated in any of the activi- *Yes No*
    ties sponsored by the Bush Faculty Devel-   1   2
    opment Program?

                                                  Yes No
11. Do you plan to participate in the future?   1   2

    IF *NO* TO QUESTION 10, GO TO QUESTION 19

12. What program(s) have you participated in?

    _____

    _____

    _____

    _____

13.   How productive was your involvement in the program?

1	2	3	4
Minimally productive	Partially productive	Moderately productive	Very productive

14.   What benefits do you feel you obtained from your participation in the program?

_____

_____

_____

_____

15.   Did your participation result in changes in   Yes   No
      your courses or teaching?   1   2

16.   Did your participation result in any publica-   Yes   No
      tions?   1   2

17a. Has participation by the faculty in the pro-   Yes   No
      gram changed the norms about teaching in   1   2
      the college (that is, amount of student writ-
      ing expected, use of discussion, student
      evaluation)?

17b. If yes please specify the changes in the norms about
      teaching?

_____

_____

_____

_____

18a. Has the program changed communication patterns in the college?

Yes No
1 2

18b. If yes please specify the changes in the communication patterns in the college.

_____

_____

_____

_____

To aid in the assessment of how different faculty groups react to faculty development, we would like to ask some information about you.

19. How long have you been a college teacher?

_____ (no. of years)

20. How long have you been a faculty member at this college/university?

_____ (no. of years)

21. Are you full-time or part-time?

Full-time Part-time
1 2

22. What is your present rank?

1 Instructor   2 Assistant Professor
3 Associate Professor   4 Professor
6 Lecturer   8 Other

23a. Do you have tenure?

Yes No
1 2

IF *NO,* GO TO QUESTION 23b

		Yes	*No*
23b.	Are you in a tenure track position?	1	2

24. In what area do you teach? _____

25. How satisfied are you with your role as a faculty member? Are you not at all, somewhat, moderately, or well satisfied? (Circle your answer.)

26. In terms of your personal experience, do you perceive the activities of research, teaching, and service as supportive or competitive with each other?

   Supportive   *Competitive*
        1   2

27. What percentage of your time would you like to spend in *teaching, service,* and *research*?

   Teaching   Service   Research

   _____   _____   _____ 100%

28. What percentage of time does the college expect you to spend in *teaching, service,* and *research*?

   _____   _____   _____ 100%

29. What percentage of time do you spend in *teaching, service,* and *research*?

   _____   _____   _____ 100%

30. In thinking about your current position, to what extent, if any, do each of the following contribute to your *satisfaction*? (Circle your answer for each item.)

    a. Job security (not at all, somewhat, considerably, a great deal)

    b. The sense of accomplishment and competence (not at all, somewhat, considerably, a great deal)

    c. The opportunity for continued learning (not at all, somewhat, considerably, a great deal)

    d. A sense of independence and autonomy (not at all, somewhat, considerably, a great deal)

    e. Support from the administration (not at all, somewhat, considerably, a great deal)

    f. Academically capable students (not at all, somewhat, considerably, a great deal)

    g. Anything else?
       (Please specify) _____

31. Now to what extent, if any, is each of the following a *concern* in your current position? (Circle your answer for each item.)

    a. Having too much to do (not at all, somewhat, conderably, a great deal)

    b. Job insecurity (not at all, somewhat, considerably, a great deal)

    c. Conflicts between teaching, scholarship, and service responsibilities (not at all, somewhat, considerably, a great deal)

d.   Lack of independence and autonomy (not at all, somewhat, considerably, a great deal)

e.   The position's monotony, routineness, or lack of challenge (not at all, somewhat, considerably, a great deal)

f.   Lack of support from the administration (not at all, somewhat, considerably, a great deal)

g.   Salary (not at all, somewhat, considerably, a great deal)

h.   Anything else?
     (Please specify) _____

Professional and Career Activities

There may be differences between what you are doing and what you want to do. We would like to list some activities you might pursue to reduce this discrepancy.

32. First, career change activities you might pursue to reduce the discrepancy between what you are doing and what you might want to do. Indicate the extent of your involvement in the following activities: (Circle your answer for each item)

a.   Looking for a different teaching position (not at all, thought about it, tried a few times, seriously involved)

b.   Looking for an administration position (not at all, thought about it, tried a few times, seriously involved)

      c.   Looking for a job outside of higher education (not at all, thought about it, tried a few times, seriously involved)

      d.   Taking early retirement (not at all, thought about it, tried a few times, seriously involved)

33.   What sort of things might sway you to seriously pursue another career?

_____

_____

_____

_____

34.   Now the scholarship activities you might pursue to reduce the discrepancy between what you are doing and what you might want to do. To what extent are you involved in the following activities: (Circle your answer for each item.)

      a.   Seeking institutional support—money for released time (not at all, thought about it, tried a few times, seriously involved)

      b.   Seeking outside funding for a project (not at all, thought about it, tried a few times, seriously involved)

      c.   Taking or sitting in on courses (not at all, thought about it, tried a few times, seriously involved)

      d.   Working on an advanced degree (not at all, thought about it, tried a few times, seriously involved)

      e.   Going to professional meetings (not at all, thought about it, tried a few times, seriously involved)

35. Now teaching activities you may be pursuing to reduce
     the discrepancy between what you are doing and what
     you might want to do. To what extent are you involved
     in the following activities: (Circle your answer for each
     item.)

     a. Attending workshops on campus (not at all, thought
         about it, tried a few times, seriously involved)

     b. Teaming with colleagues to address academic prob-
         lems (not at all, thought about it, tried a few times,
         seriously involved)

     c. Consulting with experts on teaching—for example,
         media experts (not at all, thought about it, tried a
         few times, seriously involved)

36. At what age would you like to retire? _____

37. Would you like to continue as a faculty   *Yes* *No*
     member after that age?   1   2

38. If you could continue as a faculty member after retire-
     ment age, what would you like to do?

     _____

     _____

     _____

     _____

Thank you for taking the time to complete this questionnaire.

References

"Annual Report on the Economic Status of the Profession 1983–84." *Academe: Bulletin of the American Association of University Professors,* 1984, 70 (4).

Arvin, N. *Longfellow: His Life and Work.* Boston: Little, Brown, 1963.

Baldwin, R. G. "The Changing Development Needs of an Aging Professoriate." In C. M. N. Mehrota (Ed.), *New Directions for Teaching and Learning: Teaching and Aging,* no. 19. San Francisco: Jossey-Bass, 1984.

Baldwin, R. G., and others. *Expanding Faculty Options: Career Development Projects at Colleges and Universities.* Washington, D.C.: American Association for Higher Education, 1981.

Bergquist, W. H., Phillips, S. R., and Quehl, G. *A Handbook for Faculty Development.* Vol. 1, Washington, D.C.: Council for the Advancement of Small Colleges, 1975. Vol. 2, Berkeley, Calif.: Pacific Soundings Press, 1977.

Bess, J. L. (Ed.). *New Directions for Teaching and Learning: Motivating Professors to Teach Effectively,* no. 10. San Francisco: Jossey-Bass, 1982.

Blackburn, R. T., and Havighurst, R. J. "Career Patterns of United States Male Academic Social Scientists." *Higher Education,* 1979, *8,* 553–572.

Blackburn, R. T., Pellino, G., Boberg, A., and O'Connell, C. "Are Institutional Improvement Programs Off-Target?" In *Improving Teaching and Institutional Quality.* Current Issues in Higher Education, No. 1. Washington, D.C.: American Association for Higher Education, 1980.

Broyles, S. G., and Fernandez, R. M. *Education Directory: Colleges and Universities 1983–84.* Washington, D.C.: National Center for Education Statistics, 1984.

Caplan, R. D., and others. *Job Demands and Worker Health.* Ann Arbor: Institute for Social Research, University of Michigan, 1980.

Centra, J. A. *Faculty Development Practices in U.S. Colleges and Universities.* Project Report 76–30. Princeton: Educational Testing Service, 1976.

Chait, R. P., and Ford, A. T. *Beyond Traditional Tenure: A Guide to Sound Policies and Practices.* San Francisco: Jossey-Bass, 1982.

Clark, S. M., Corcoran, M., and Lewis, D. R. "Critical Perspectives on Faculty Career Development with Implications for Differentiated Institutional Policies." Paper presented at the meeting of the American Educational Research Association, New Orleans, La., 1984.

Cross, K. P. *Accent on Learning: Improving Instruction and Reshaping the Curriculum.* San Francisco: Jossey-Bass, 1976.

Cross, K. P. "Two Scenarios for Higher Education's Future." *American Association of Higher Education Bulletin,* 1980, *33* (1), 11–17.

Deci, E. L., and Ryan, R. M. "Intrinsic Motivation to Teach: Possibilities and Obstacles in Our Universities." In J. L. Bess (Ed.), *New Directions for Teaching and Learning: Motivating Professors to Teach Effectively,* no. 10. San Francisco: Jossey-Bass, 1982.

Eble, K. E. *Professors as Teachers.* San Francisco: Jossey-Bass, 1972.

Eble, K. E. *The Craft of Teaching: A Guide to Mastering the Professor's Art.* San Francisco: Jossey-Bass, 1976.

Eckert, R. E., and Stecklein, J. E. *Job Motivations and Satisfactions of College Teachers: A Study of Faculty Members in Minnesota Colleges.* Washington, D.C.: U.S. Government Printing Office, 1961.

Fact-File, "Universities Ranked Among the Top 500 Defense Contractors in Fiscal 1983." *Chronicle of Higher Education,* August 1, 1984, p. 14.

Fink, L. D. (Ed.). *New Directions for Teaching and Learning: The First Year of College Teaching,* no. 17. San Francisco: Jossey-Bass, 1984.

Foster, S. F., and Nelson, J. C. "Five Year Follow-Up on Needs and Means for University Teaching Improvement: Canadian Survey IV." In T. B. Massey (Ed.), *Proceedings of the Tenth International Conference on Improving University Teaching.* College Park: University of Maryland University College, 1984.

Frances, C. *College Enrollment Trends: Testing the Conventional Wisdom Against the Facts.* Washington, D.C.: American Council on Education, 1980.

French, J. R. P., Jr., Tupper, C. J., and Mueller, E. F. "Work Load of University Professors." Unpublished manuscript. Center for Research on Learning and Teaching, University of Michigan, 1965.

Gaff, J. G. *Toward Faculty Renewal: Advances in Faculty, Instructional, and Organizational Development.* San Francisco: Jossey-Bass, 1975.

Gaff, J. G., and Morstain, B. R. "Evaluating the Outcomes." In J. G. Gaff (Ed.), *New Directions for Higher Education: Institutional Renewal Through the Improvement of Teaching,* no. 24. San Francisco: Jossey-Bass, 1978.

Gaff, S. S., Festa, C., and Gaff, J. G. *Professional Development: A Guide to Resources.* New Rochelle, N.Y.: *Change* Magazine Press, 1978.

Grant, W. V., and Snyder, T. D. *Digest of Education Statistics,*

1983-84. Washington, D.C.: National Center for Education Statistics, 1983.

Group for Human Development in Higher Education. *Faculty Development in a Time of Retrenchment.* New Rochelle, N.Y.: *Change* Magazine Press, 1974.

Gustad, J. W. *The Career Decisions of College Teachers.* Washington, D.C.: U.S. Department of Health, Education, and Welfare, 1960.

Ingraham, M. P. *The Outer Fringe: Faculty Benefits Other Than Annuities and Insurance.* Madison: University of Wisconsin Press, 1965.

Jacobson, R. L. "AAUP's Leader Assays Decline in Faculty Morale, Governance." *Chronicle of Higher Education,* June 27, 1984, pp. 15, 17.

Kanter, R. M. "Changing the Shape of Work: Reform in Academe." *Current Issues in Higher Education,* 1979, *1,* 3-10.

Kohlberg, L. *The Philosophy of Moral Development.* San Francisco: Harper & Row, 1982.

Lacey, P. A. (Ed.). *New Directions for Teaching and Learning: Revitalizing Teaching Through Faculty Development,* no. 15. San Francisco: Jossey-Bass, 1983.

Levinson, D. J., and others. *The Seasons of a Man's Life.* New York: Knopf, 1978.

Light, D. "Thinking About Faculty." *Daedalus,* 1984, *103,* 258-264.

Lindquist, J. (Ed.). *Designing Teaching Improvement Programs.* Washington, D.C.: Council for the Advancement of Small Colleges, 1979.

Maehr, M. L. "The Professor of the Future: Expectations, Dilemmas, Solutions." In T. B. Massey (Ed.), *Proceedings of the Tenth International Conference on Improving University Teaching.* College Park: University of Maryland University College, 1984.

Marsh, H. W. "Validity of Students' Evaluations of College Teaching: A Multitrait-Multimethod Analysis." *Journal of Educational Psychology,* 1982, *74,* 264-279.

Mayer, R. E. *Thinking, Problem Solving, Cognition.* New York: W. H. Freeman, 1983.

Miller, W. S., and Wilson, K. M. *Faculty Development Proce-*

dures in Small Colleges: A Southern Survey. Atlanta, Ga.: Southern Regional Education Board, 1963.

Nelsen, W. C. *Renewal of the Teacher Scholar: Faculty Development in the Liberal Arts College.* Washington, D.C.: Association of American Colleges, 1981.

Nelsen, W. C., and Siegel, M. E. (Eds.). *Effective Approaches to Faculty Development.* Washington, D.C.: Association of American Colleges, 1980.

Pelz, D. C., and Andrews, F. M. *Scientists in Organizations.* (Rev. ed.) Ann Arbor: Institute for Social Research, University of Michigan, 1976.

Perry, W. G., Jr. *Forms of Intellectual and Ethical Development in the College Years.* New York: Holt, Rinehart and Winston, 1970.

Quinn, R. P., Staines, G., and McCullough, M. *Job Satisfaction: Is There a Trend?* Manpower Research Monograph, No. 30. Washington, D.C.: U.S. Department of Labor, 1974.

Rudolph, F. *Curriculum: A History of the Undergraduate Course of Study Since 1636.* San Francisco: Jossey-Bass, 1977.

Siegel, M. E. "Empirical Findings on Faculty Development Pro grams." In W. C. Nelsen and M. E. Siegel (Eds.), *Effective Approaches to Faculty Development.* Washington, D.C.: Association of American Colleges, 1980.

Smith, A. B. *Faculty Development and Evaluation in Higher Education.* ERIC/Higher Education Research Report No. 8. Washington, D.C.: American Association for Higher Education, 1976.

Smith, B. *A Profile of Faculty Participating in Instructional Workshops at the University of Michigan.* Ann Arbor: Center for Research on Learning and Teaching, University of Michigan, 1981.

Snyder, R. A., and Morris, J. H. "Organizational Communication and Performance." *Journal of Applied Psychology,* 1984, *69* (3), 461–465.

Stecklein, J. E., Willie, R., and Lorenz, G. E. *The Minnesota College Teacher Study.* Minneapolis: University of Minnesota, 1983.

Watkins, B. T. "Concern over Departments' Resources Found

Widespread Among Professors." *Chronicle of Higher Education,* November 23, 1983, p. 19.

White, E. *Teaching and Assessing Writing: Recent Advances in Understanding, Evaluating, and Improving Student Performance.* San Francisco: Jossey-Bass, 1985.

Wilson, R. C. *Using Consultation to Improve Teaching.* Berkeley: University of California Innovation and Evaluation Services, 1984.

Wilson, R. C., and others. *College Professors and Their Impact on Students.* New York: Wiley, 1975.

Index